# THE MAHABHARATA

# The Mahabharata

## A PLAY

### Based Upon the Indian Classic Epic

*by* JEAN-CLAUDE CARRIÈRE

*Translated from the French*

*by* PETER BROOK

*A Cornelia & Michael Bessie Book*

HARPER & ROW, PUBLISHERS, New York
Cambridge, Philadelphia, San Francisco, Washington
London, Mexico City, São Paulo, Singapore, Sydney

For Marie-Hélène Estienne
who has held the threads
of The Mahabharata together
through two languages,
four continents, eight years

*Designer: Sidney Feinberg*

*Copyeditor: Brian Hotchkiss*

Library of Congress Cataloging-in-Publication Data

Carrière, Jean Claude.
  The Mahabharata.
  Play adapted from the Indian epic.
  "A Cornelia & Michael Bessie book."
  I. Mahabharata. II. Title.
PQ2663.A78M3413      1987      842'.914   87-45025
ISBN 0-06-039072-7            87 88 89 90 91 MPC 10 9 8 7 6 5 4 3 2 1
ISBN 0-06-039079-4 (pbk.)     87 88 89 90 91 MPC 10 9 8 7 6 5 4 3 2

# CONTENTS

# INTRODUCTION

———◈———

## by Jean-Claude Carrière

*The Mahabharata* is one of the world's greatest books. It is also the longest poem ever written. It was written in Sanskrit, and is more than a hundred thousand stanzas long—about fifteen times the length of the Bible.

The first known written versions of it, made up of ancient stories, go back to the fifth or sixth century B.C. These versions continued to be made for seven or eight hundred years, until in the third or fourth century A.D., they took on a more or less definitive form. All during this time of composition additions of all kinds were made—up until the twentieth century—with variations depending on the province of origin, traditions, interpretations, or the various groups of writers involved.

In the Indian tradition, *The Mahabharata* is simply called "The Epic," and it is the masterpiece of the very rich literature of the Sanskrit language. The poem is at the origin of thousands of beliefs, legends, thoughts, teachings, and characters which even today are part of Indian life.

Yet it was entirely unknown in Europe until the eighteenth century. The first edition of the "Bhagavad Gita," a section of the poem, was published in London in 1785 in a translation by Charles Wilkins, and in Paris in 1787, translated into French by M. Parraud. The first European to immerse himself in the entire poem was a Swiss Army officer of French extraction, Colonel de Polier, who lived thirty adventurous years in India, also in the late eighteenth century. In the nineteenth century a French orientalist, Hippolyte Fauche, undertook the colossal task of translating the whole epic into French. Only two hundred people subscribed to buy the work. After many long years of labor, Fauche died. His work was taken up by Dr. L. Ballin, who also died before it was finished. But this translation, which is very beautiful in many ways, is often incorrect or incomprehensible. In any case, it is incomplete. There is no complete French version of the world's greatest poem.

One evening in 1975 Philippe Lavastine, a remarkable professor of Sanskrit, began telling the first stories of *The Mahabharata* to Peter Brook and me. We were completely enchanted. For five years we met regularly, Peter and I listening to the poem without reading it. I took notes, and in 1976 I started a first version of the play.

Advice and encouragement came from a number of quarters, particularly from Madeleine Biardeau, author of several works on Hindu culture, and finally we began to read. At first we read separately; Peter Brook read in English and I read in French, and finally we began a long, slow study together, comparing translations, with the help of Marie-Hélène Estienne. After these studies, which we pursued for almost two years, we traveled to India a number of times. We gathered all kinds of images and impressions—images of dance, film, marionette theatre, village celebrations and plays.

Although, so far as we know, there has never been a complete adaptation of *The Mahabharata* (the filmmaker Satyajit Ray worked on one for many years, but had to give up for lack of funds), many episodes of the epic poem are very alive today in both India and Indonesia. They are often played, in a variety of fashions, and the stories are told in picture form, which can be found all over the country.

We read a great deal during this time of research, and some of it was most revealing. I'm thinking particularly of several short plays by Rabindranath Tagore, freely adapted from the epic, a brilliant essay by Iravati Karve called "Yuganta," and a long series of the Krishnavatara (the "descent" of Krishna) edited by K. M. Munshi, all of which gave us precious keys to meanings, and made possible a more subtle, deeper and in a way more realistic development of certain characters.

The Indians with whom we talked about our project responded warmly, once they were over their initial amazement. The notion that their great Indian epic would at last be played in the West intrigued and interested them. We received the advice of professors and the benediction of saints. In Calcutta we met a hospitable and enthusiastic man, Professor P. Lal, who was finishing a complete translation into English verse of *The Mahabharata*, which he called a "transcreation." He too was most encouraging, convinced that the great Indian poem could speak in different voices to the rest of the world.

"Maha" in Sanskrit means "great" or "complete." A maharajah is a great king. "Bharata" is first of all the name of a legendary character, then that of a family or a clan. So the title can be understood as "The Great History of the Bharatas." But in an extended meaning, bharata means Hindu, and even more generally, man. So it can also be interpreted as "The Great History of Mankind."

This "great poem of the world" tells the story of the long and bloody quarrel between two groups of cousins: the Pandavas, who were five brothers; and the Kauravas, of whom there were a hundred. This family quarrel over who will rule ends with an enormous battle where the fate of the world is at stake.

The events told in *The Mahabharata* most probably have a historic source. Most specialists are agreed on this point. Indian tradition places the great battle of Kurukshetra in the year 3200 B.C. Some historians see in the poem a reasonably faithful reflection of the wars between the Dravidians and the Aryans of the second millennium B.C. Others maintain that the correct interpretation of the poem is entirely mythological. Still others point out the importance of the teaching books of the epic—political, social, moral and religious— and see *The Mahabharata* as a long treatise of royal initiation.

Commentators point out that all the pages that maintain the superi-

ority of the Brahman caste—and there are a great number of them—
were added in a much more recent time.

We didn't pay a great deal of attention to any of these comments,
however interesting they might be. As far as we were concerned, this
immense poem, which flows with the majesty of a great river, carries
an inexhaustible richness which defies all structural, thematic, historic or psychological analysis. Doors are constantly opening which
lead to other doors. It is impossible to hold *The Mahabharata* in the
palm of your hand. Layers of ramifications, sometimes contradictory,
follow upon one another and are interwoven without losing the
central theme. That theme is a threat: we live in a time of destruction—everything points in the same direction. Can this destruction
be avoided?

I began the final draft in autumn 1982. I continued throughout
1983 as well as 1984, when research began with the actors, as well
as the music composition.

When rehearsals began, in September 1984, the play was written,
but there was as yet no definitive structure. Throughout the nine
months of rehearsal, incessant changes were made. For a long time
we had no idea how lengthy the play would be, how many playing
hours we would need, or how many plays were involved.

From the beginning it seemed obvious that we would have to set
aside most of the secondary strands of the story, although many of
them are very beautiful. The storytellers of *The Mahabharata* liked to
arrest the mainstream of the action for a while to tell another story,
like a little backwater, which illustrates or comments upon the main
action. Some of these stories go on for over fifty pages; for instance,
the rivalry between Drona and Draupadi, or the loves of Nala and
Damayanti. Some are shorter, such as the cunning and courageous
Savitri's snatching her husband from death. Some, on the other hand,
take only a single page—the loves of Arjuna and the daughter of the
king of snakes. *The Mahabharata* even contains a shorter version of
the other great Sanskrit epic, the *Ramayana*.

At various times we tried a very dramatic beginning, in the middle of the conflict. But each time it seemed to us that the fabled origins of the family, the adventures and desires of faraway mythic ancestors, were absolutely necessary, even if that meant forty minutes of playing time before the appearance of the principal characters. It became obvious that we needed the storyteller/author, Vyasa, even though the characters he creates sometimes escape him (he is both their author and their father), and even though Ganesha and later Krishna dispute the reality of his inventions.

Eventually a clear line began to appear, which led from a mythic tale of demigods told by a storyteller, to characters who became more and more human and who brought with them the theatre as we understand it.

In *The Mahabharata* there are sixteen main characters. Each of them has a distinct and often complex personality and a particular story which is part of the main action, with varying degrees of importance. We left out only one of these, Vidura, half brother of Pandu and Dhritarashtra, but a half brother born of a servant and consequently unable to exercise royal power. Vidura is a wise, moderate, sensible man whose effect on the plot is minor. What he brings to the poem, and it is almost always a purely verbal contribution, has been incorporated into other characters: Bhishma, Yudhishthira or Vyasa himself.

Krishna presented us with a special problem. Today it is almost impossible to separate Krishna from his immense later legend, which kept developing up to the Middle Ages. But in *The Mahabharata*, at least in those parts of the poem generally thought to be the earliest, nothing clearly indicates that he is an avatar, one of the earthly incarnations of Vishnu. He is a man who tires, who ages. Sometimes he is "surprised" or "distressed" by the things that happen. Mysterious and bloody revolts destroy his city. And he dies killed by a hunter in the forest—an abrupt death, briefly told.

Some commentators, such as Norbert Klaes in "Conscience and

Consciousness," maintain that in the original *Mahabharata* Krishna is simply Vasudeva, the best and highest of men, of whom only one is alive at any given moment. Not a god.

Yet the poem describes some of his prodigious acts. Krishna lengthens Draupadi's dress indefinitely. He creates an illusion which makes his enemies believe that the sun has set before its time. He possesses an invincible weapon, a disc, which he uses to decapitate Sisupala. But above all, just before the battle he gives his friend Arjuna the "Bhagavad Gita," the famous text where he appears as a divinity and shows his "universal form."

Man or god? It is obviously not up to us to decide. Any historical or theological truth, controversial by its very nature, is closed to us—our aim is a certain dramatic truth. This is why we have chosen to keep the two faces of Krishna that are in the original poem, and to emphasize their opposite and paradoxical nature.

In order to adapt *The Mahabharata,* to transform an immense epic poem into a play, or three plays, we had to draw new scenes from our imaginations, bring together characters who never meet in the poem itself. All this within the context of deep respect for the shape and sense of the story. Each of these characters has a total commitment, each probes in depth the nature of his actions, each considers his dharma, and each confronts his idea of fate. So we had to make it possible for each of these characters to go into his own deepest places without interposing our concepts, our judgments or our twentieth-century analysis, insofar as that is possible.

In the second play, which involves long years of exile, we had to find some way of concentrating fast and fluid action in space and time without destroying its energy or its mystery.

As far as the writing itself is concerned, we dropped the notion of archaic or old-fashioned languages, because they carry with them a trail of inappropriate images of our own Middle Ages or ancient tales. On the other hand, it was impossible to tell this story in modern, familiar or even slangy language. But the polish of French classic or neoclassic language was, of course, equally impossible. So we settled on a simple, precise, restrained language which gave us the means to oppose or juxtapose words which ordinarily are never used together.

This careful choice of language led us to a problem which would be repeated in the stage decor, the music, the costumes, the colors, and the props: one might call it "the Indian-ness." I had to write in French without writing a French play. I had to open my language to rhythms and images of the East without being caught in the other trap, the opposite one, of providing local color or the picturesque.

While we kept the names of characters, we found equivalents for most of the Sanskrit words. There were two exceptions: one was Kshatriya. In ancient India it was the name of a caste, which is untranslatable unless one attempts a kind of forcible assimilation which would be a colonization by vocabulary—words like "noble" or "warrior" and certainly "knight" simply would not do. The other untranslatable word is dharma, a concept at the very heart of the poem: "truth," "justice," or "duty" fall short of the mark. Dharma is the law on which rests the order of the world. Dharma is also the personal and secret order each human being recognizes as his own, the law he must obey. And the dharma of the individual, if it is respected, is the warrant of its faithful reflection of a cosmic order.

Indian tradition says: "Everything in *The Mahabharata* is elsewhere. What is not there is nowhere."

# FOREWORD

◆

## by Peter Brook

One of the difficulties we encounter when we see traditional theatre from the East is that we admire without understanding. Unless we possess the keys to the symbols, we remain on the outside, fascinated, perhaps, by the surface, but unable to contact the human realities without which these complex art forms would never have arisen.

The day I first saw a demonstration of Kathakali, I heard a word completely new to me—*The Mahabharata*. A dancer was presenting a scene from this work and his sudden first appearance from behind a curtain was an unforgettable shock. His costume was red and gold, his face was red and green, his nose was like a white billiard ball, his fingernails were like knives; in place of beard and mustache, two white crescent moons thrust forward from his lips, his eyebrows shot up and down like drumsticks and his fingers spelled out strange coded messages. Through the magnificent ferocity of the movements, I could see that a story was unfolding. But what story? I could only guess at something mythical and remote, from another culture, nothing to do with my life.

Gradually, sadly, I realized that my interest was lessening, the visual shock was wearing off. However, after the interval, the dancer returned without his makeup, no longer a demigod, just a likable Indian in shirt and jeans. He described the scene he had been playing and repeated the dance. The hieratic gestures passed through the man of today. The superb, but impenetrable image had given way to an ordinary, more accessible one and I realized that I preferred it this way.

When I next encountered *The Mahabharata*, it was as a series of

stories told to Jean-Claude Carrière and me with passionate enthusi-
asm by a remarkable Sanskrit scholar, Philippe Lavastine. Through
him we began to understand why this was one of the greatest works
of humanity, and how, like all great works, it is both far from us and
very near. It contains the most profound expressions of Hindu
thought, and yet for over two thousand years it has penetrated so
intimately into the daily life of India that for many millions of people
the characters are eternally alive—as real as members of their own
family, with whom they share the quarrels and the questions.

Jean-Claude and I were so fascinated that standing in the rue St.
André des Arts at three o'clock in the morning after a long storytell-
ing session, we made a mutual commitment. We would find a way
of bringing this material into our world and sharing these stories with
an audience in the West.

Once we had taken this decision, the first step was obviously to go
to India. Here began a long series of journeys in which gradually all
those preparing the project took part—actors, musicians, designers.
India ceased to be a dream and we became infinitely the richer. I
cannot say that we saw all its aspects, but we saw enough to learn
that its variety is infinite. Every day brought a new surprise and a
new discovery.

We saw that for several thousand years India has lived in a climate
of constant creativity. Even if life flows with the majestic slowness
of a great river, at the same time, within the current, each atom has
its own dynamic energy. Whatever the aspect of human experience,
the Indian has indefatigably explored every possibility. If it is that
most humble and most amazing of human instruments, a finger,
everything that a finger can do has been explored and codified. If it
is a word, a breath, a limb, a sound, a note—or a stone or a color or
a cloth—all its aspects, practical, artistic and spiritual, have been
investigated and linked together. Art means celebrating the most
refined possibilities of every element, and art means extracting the
essence from every detail so that the detail can reveal itself as a
meaningful part of an inseparable whole. The more we saw of Indian

classical art forms, especially in the performing arts, the more we realized that they take at least a lifetime to master, and that a foreigner can only admire, not imitate.

The line between performance and ceremony is hard to draw, and we witnessed many events that took us close to Vedic times, or close to the energy that is uniquely Indian. Theyyems, Mudiattu, Yakshagana, Chaau, Jatra—every region has its form of drama and almost every form—sung, mimed, narrated—touches or tells a part of *Mahabharata*. Wherever we went, we met sages, scholars, villagers, pleased to find foreigners interested in their great epic and generously happy to share their understanding.

We were touched by the love that Indians bring to *The Mahabharata*, and this filled us both with respect and awe at the task we had assumed.

Yet we knew that theatre must not be solemn and we must not allow ourselves to become crushed into a false reverence. What guided us most in India was the popular tradition. Here we recognized the techniques that all folk art has in common and which we have explored in improvisations over the years. We have always considered a theatre group as a multi-headed storyteller, and one of the most fascinating ways of meeting *The Mahabharata* in India is through the storyteller. He not only plays on his musical instrument, but uses it as a unique scenic device to suggest a bow, a sword, a mace, a river, an army or a monkey's tail.

We returned from India knowing that our work was not to imitate but to suggest.

Jean-Claude then began the vast undertaking of turning all these experiences into a text. There were times when I saw his mind reaching explosion point, because of the multitude of impressions and the innumerable units of information he had stored over the years. On the first day of rehearsal, Jean-Claude said to the actors as he handed them nine hours' worth of text: "Don't take this to be a finished play. Now I'm going to start rewriting each scene as we see it evolve in your hands." In fact, he didn't rewrite every scene, but the material was constantly developing as we worked.

Then we decided to make an English version and I set out to prepare a translation that would be as faithful as possible to Jean-Claude's gigantic labor.

In the performance, whether in English or French, we are not attempting a reconstruction of Dravidian and Aryan India of three thousand years ago. We are not presuming to present the symbolism of Hindu philosophy. In the music, in the costumes, in the movements, we have tried to suggest the flavor of India without pretending to be what we are not. On the contrary, the many nationalities who have gathered together are trying to reflect *The Mahabharata* by bringing to it something of their own. In this way, we are trying to celebrate a work which only India could have created but which carries echoes for all mankind.

PART I

THE GAME
OF DICE

# THE BEGINNINGS

*A boy of about twelve enters. He goes toward a little pool. Then a man appears. He is thin, wearing a muddy loincloth, his feet bare and dirty. He sits thoughtfully on the ground and, noticing the boy, he signals him to come closer. The boy approaches, slightly fearful. The man asks him:*

VYASA: Do you know how to write?

BOY: No, why? *The man is silent for a moment before saying:*

VYASA: I've composed a great poem. I've composed it all, but nothing is written. I need someone to write down what I know.

BOY: What's your name?

VYASA: Vyasa.

BOY: What's your poem about?

VYASA: It's about you.

BOY: Me?

VYASA: Yes, it's the story of your race, how your ancestors were born, how they grew up, how a vast war arose. It's the poetical history of mankind. If you listen carefully, at the end you'll be someone else. For it's as pure as glass, yet nothing is omitted. It washes away faults, it sharpens the brain and it gives long life. *Suddenly the boy points, indicating a strange form approaching in the distance.*

BOY: Who's that? *It is someone with an elephant's head and a man's body, who comes strutting toward them. He has writing materials in his hand. Vyasa greets him warmly.*

3

VYASA: Ganesha! Welcome.

BOY: You're Ganesha?

GANESHA: Rumor has it that you're looking for a scribe for the Poetical History of Mankind. I'm at your service.

BOY: You're really Ganesha?

GANESHA: In person.

BOY: Why do you have an elephant's head?

GANESHA: Don't you know?

BOY: No.

GANESHA: If I've got to tell my story too, we'll never finish.

BOY: Please.

GANESHA: Right. I am the son of Parvati, the wife of Shiva.

BOY: The wife of the great god, Shiva?

GANESHA: Himself. But Shiva's not my father. My mother did it alone.

BOY: How did she manage?

GANESHA: It's not easy. You need some earth, a pinch of safran, a few drops of dew. To cut a long story short, when I arrived in this world, I was already a fine, sturdy boy, just about your age. One day, my mother told me to guard the door of the house. She wanted to take a bath. "Let no one in," she said. An instant later, Shiva was standing in front of me, wanting to come into the house, his house. I blocked the way. Shiva did not know me—I'd only just been born—so he said "Out of my way! It's an order. This is my home." I answered, "My mother told me to let no one in so I'm letting no one in." Shiva was furious. He called up his most ferocious cohorts. He commanded them to flush me out, but I sent them flying. My force was superhuman. I blazed, I glittered, I exploded—horde after horde of demons withdrew in shame, for I was defending my mother. Shiva had only one way left: cunning. He slipped behind me and suddenly he chopped off my head. My mother's anger had no limits. She threatened to destroy all the powers of heaven and smash the sky into tiny splinters. Shiva, to calm her down, ordered a head to be put on me as quickly as possible, the head of the first creature to come by. It was an elephant. So there we are. I'm Ganesha, the bringer of peace. *He positions himself with great care and says to Vyasa:* I'm ready. You can begin. But I warn you: my hand can't stop once I start to write. You must dictate without a single pause.

VYASA: And you, before putting anything down, you must understand the sense of what I say.

GANESHA: Count on me. *A silence falls and lasts a few moments.* We're expecting someone?

VYASA: No.

GANESHA: So . . . ?

VYASA: There's something secret about a beginning. I don't know how to start.

GANESHA: May I offer a suggestion?

VYASA: You're most welcome.

GANESHA: As you claim to be the author of the poem, how about beginning with yourself?

VYASA: Right. A king, hunting in a forest, fell asleep. He dreamed of his wife and there was a joyful explosion of sperm.

GANESHA: Very good start.

VYASA: When the king awoke and saw the sperm on a leaf, he called a falcon and said, "Take my sperm quickly to the queen." But the falcon was attacked by another falcon, the sperm fell into a river, a fish swallowed it. A few months later, a fisherman caught the fish, cut it open and found in its stomach a tiny little girl, whom he called Satyavati. She grew up. She became very beautiful, but unfortunately she smelled most dreadfully of fish. This made her very sad; no one would come near her. Then, one day, she met a wandering hermit who said to her: "I like you. Let's make love, here, right away, and I promise I'll turn your dreadful stench into a most delicious odor." She cried: "Now! Here! In broad daylight! I can't!" So the hermit drew a thick mist across the river and fields, he took her to an island, she opened herself to him and as she did so she became fragrant, irresistible. . . .

BOY: They had a son?

VYASA: Yes. I am that son. Vyasa. And Satyavati went back to the fisherman, whom she called her father.

GANESHA: Keep going, son of the mist. We haven't yet started. What happened at the beginning?

VYASA: In those days, the king was called Santanu. One day, he was walking beside the river when suddenly there appeared before him a woman of a beauty that beggars description. *Vyasa himself bows to a woman (Ganga) who has just appeared.*

VYASA–SANTANU: "You take my breath away," he told her. Wonder blows my mind. Whoever you are, creature of darkness or spirit of the sky, be mine.

GANGA: Do you accept my conditions?

VYASA–SANTANU: At once. What are they?

GANGA: You will never challenge my actions, nor oppose them, whether you find them good or bad. You will be neither curious nor angry and you will never ask the slightest question, on pain of seeing me leave you instantly.

VYASA–SANTANU: I accept. Come.

GANGA: I come.

VYASA: They lived a year of boundless love. A child was born. His mother wrapped him in a piece of cloth, cried:

GANGA: I love you!

VYASA: And laughing, threw him into the river. "Don't ask!" Santanu told himself "I must never ask a question." The next year they had another child. She cried:

GANGA: I love you!

VYASA: And drowned it. "Don't ask!" Santanu repeated. And so it went, for seven years. The eighth year, an eighth child was born.

GANGA: I love you! *Ganga prepares to drown her eighth child. Santanu cannot hold himself back any longer. He cries out.*

VYASA–SANTANU: Stop! Stop! Why these murders? Why are you killing these children?

GANGA: Why? I am Ganga. I am goddess of this river. I didn't kill these children, I saved them. Like me, they were of divine origin, but condemned to be born and die again amongst men. I agreed to set them free and that is why I laughed. Now I must go. This eighth child will be called Bhishma. He will be infallible, invincible. Farewell.

VYASA–SANTANU: And the goddess vanished.

BOY: What happened to the child?

VYASA: She took him away. The world knew twenty years of happiness. Santanu reigned with perfect justice, there was no war, no misery—it was a golden age. One morning, twenty years later, he was taking his customary walk beside the river when suddenly, bubbling and churning, the water opened and out of it rose a resplendent young man, armed to the teeth.

Boy: Bhishma?

Vyasa: Yes. Santanu recognized his son and called the goddess: "Ganga! Ganga!" She appeared, robed in a fountain of foam. *The goddess is there again, she says to Santanu:*

Ganga: Here is Bhishma, our eighth child. I brought him up, taught him everything and now his knowledge matches his strength. Take him. He is yours.

Vyasa: Santanu returned to the palace with his son. Everyone admired him and saw in him the future king, a wonder king. But another day, when King Santanu was taking his melancholy promenade by the river—for he went back there every day—all at once the air was filled with an enchanting fragrance. The king followed the scent and saw before him a woman of wondrous beauty. *Once more, Santanu finds a beautiful woman crossing his path.*

Vyasa–Santanu: Who are you?

Satyavati: I'm Satyavati. My father is king of the fishermen.

Boy: Satyavati? Your mother?

Vyasa: Yes, my mother.

Ganesha: Your mother's going to play a part in your story?

Vyasa: Any objection?

Ganesha: No objection at all. Go on.

Vyasa: So Santanu fell on his knees and said to the sweet-scented maiden: *Vyasa goes down on one knee and addresses the woman:* "I've been a widower for many years. I've held down my heart and watched over my people. But now the blow of your scent sends me reeling, it blends with the blood in my veins. I'm caught in its silken net. Satyavati, be my bride."

SATYAVATI: My hand belongs to my father. *As she speaks, the king of the fishermen appears.*

KING OF THE FISHERMEN: Santanu, there's no doubt my daughter needs a husband and you are a most worthy match. But in exchange I need a promise: the child you make together will succeed to your throne.

VYASA: That's not possible, said Santanu. I already have a son, a perfect son. He's young, he's strong—he's the future king.

KING OF THE FISHERMEN: If that's the case, farewell. Go back to your palace, forget my daughter. *The king of the fishermen and Satyavati begin to go. Bhishma calls after them.*

BHISHMA: Wait! You have just killed my father. Accept this marriage. At my request.

KING OF THE FISHERMEN: Bhishma, you are the best of sons, the noblest of heroes. We see you everywhere, arms in hand and no one dares say you no. Your enemies tremble for their lives. Whether I give you my daughter or refuse her, the danger is the same.

BHISHMA: What danger?

KING OF THE FISHERMEN: If I refuse, I foresee your fury. If I give her to your father, they will have children, children who will be your rivals, whom you will grow to hate.

BHISHMA: I make a solemn oath; the son your daughter bears will be our king.

KING OF THE FISHERMEN: You give up all your rights?

BHISHMA: Yes. Forever.

KING OF THE FISHERMEN: You surprise me.

BHISHMA: I give you my word.

KING OF THE FISHERMEN: Bhishma, I speak to you from my heart, as a father. Listen carefully. I do not doubt your word, not for a second, but if one day you have children, what will they make of your vow? They will be strong like you. If they want to conquer the kingdom by force, who could resist them?

BHISHMA: I understand and I reassure you. To avoid all conflict, and for love of my father, I swear the oath of absolute renunciation. I will say it clearly. I abjure forever the love of woman.

KING OF THE FISHERMEN: Say again what you have just said.

BHISHMA: I abjure forever the love of woman.

BOY: He said that?

VYASA: He said just that, in all solemnity. At once, voices rang through the sky, crying "Bhishma! Bhishma!" and flowers rained upon the earth.

*Bhishma takes Satyavati by the hand and leads her to his father.*

BHISHMA: Climb on my chariot, mother. I will take you to the palace.

GANESHA: Did Bhishma like women?

VYASA: No one ever knew. But as a reward for his vow, he was given the power to choose the time of his death.

BOY: Is it possible?

VYASA: It was possible in those days.

GANESHA: And then?

VYASA: Twenty years went by. Santanu and Satyavati had a son, but the heir to the throne was a poor weakling. Santanu died.

GANESHA: Like us all. And Bhishma remained without a wife?

VYASA: Yes. Passionately faithful to his vow. But you know, in the olden days if a king wanted to get married, he had to win a wife in a tournament. The little king was far too feeble to take part, so Bhishma fought in his place. He swept everyone off the field and came back with three wives instead of one.

*Bhishma reappears leading three princesses.*

GANESHA: What are you doing with three wives? Didn't you swear to abjure all women?

BHISHMA: They are not for my narrow bed. No, I haven't broken my vow. They are for the young king, my father's son.

BOY: What are their names?

BHISHMA: Amba, Ambika, and Ambalika.

BOY: Amba's crying. *The boy points to one of the princesses who is indeed crying.*

BHISHMA: You're right. Amba, why these tears?

AMBA: Listen to me, Bhishma. Before you won me at the tournament, I had already chosen a husband in secret. He knows it and he loves me. It's King Salva. How can you—who so revere fidelity—how can you marry me to your half-brother when I'm already bound by love to another man? Salva is waiting for me. Let me join him.

*Bhishma has a moment's reflection before replying:*

BHISHMA: What you say is true, Amba. You can go. *A young king is there; Amba runs toward him. As he sees her, he starts laughing. Amba is disconcerted.*

AMBA: Salva . . .

SALVA: What?

AMBA: It's me, Amba. Why are you laughing?

SALVA: So Bhishma let you go?

AMBA: Yes.

SALVA: Go back to him, Amba. I don't want you anymore.

AMBA: What are you saying?

SALVA: You're his prize. You're soiled. I couldn't for anything in the world let someone else's woman penetrate into my palace.

AMBA: But I'm not his. He has never touched me. Not grazed me with the back of his hand. He has not even wanted me. Salva, I'm a virgin and my eyes know only you.

SALVA: Please leave.

AMBA: I can't. Where could I go?

SALVA: I repeat, I don't want you anymore. Bhishma scares me and you are his prize. You no longer exist. Go away.

*Amba calls wildly:*

AMBA: Bhishma! *Bhishma is there.*

BHISHMA: What now?

AMBA: Save me. I've been rejected by the man I love and you are the cause of my misery. You can't abandon me now. You won me. I'm your wife. Marry me.

BHISHMA: You know I can't marry you, Amba. No women can come into my life. As Salva has rejected you, you are free. Go back to your father.

AMBA: No, I'm not free and I refuse to go back to my father, who bartered me like an animal. Listen. Hear what I'll do. I will walk straight ahead, in ripped clothes, begging my way, and I will live with one thought, only one, night and day, only one, a thought like a blade: how to find someone to fight you to your death.

BHISHMA: No one can kill me. It's impossible.

AMBA: I will do so, all the same. Yes, I too pronounce a vow: in one of the worlds, I will find your executioner. There's now on this earth a woman who will always think of you. Never forget me, Bhishma. I am your death. *Amba leaves. Bhishma watches her go in silence. Now, Satyavati reappears, she is sobbing.*

SATYAVATI: Bhishma! Bhishma!

BHISHMA: What is it?

SATYAVATI: The king my son is dead. *A moment's silence.*

GANESHA: Did he die without children?

VYASA: Of course. He died on his wedding day.

GANESHA: So there are no more descendants.

VYASA: No. Not one.

GANESHA: But without children this story cannot go on.

VYASA: Exactly.

GANESHA: It's absolutely necessary to give children to the princesses.

VYASA: Yes. Legitimate children.

BHISHMA: Who could father these children?

GANESHA: Why, you, of course, Bhishma. You're the only one.

BHISHMA: No. I cannot break my vow.

GANESHA: The destiny of a race is at stake. You can surely forget your vow, just for once.

BHISHMA: Ganesha, this vow is the pillar of my life. Night after night I've fought against the temptation to break it and I have triumphed. Today I'm over fifty. Breaking my vow would be worse than death, it would kill my soul. I don't want another word on the subject.

GANESHA: So the poetical history of mankind is already over. I'll collect my bits and pieces and be off. *Ganesha is starting to pack his writing materials when Satyavati suddenly says:*

SATYAVATI: No, wait a moment. Don't go. *She goes to Vyasa.* Vyasa, you are forgetting someone who can give children to the princesses.

VYASA: Who?

SATYAVATI: You. You, Vyasa.

GANESHA: And why Vyasa? Where does this idea come from?

BHISHMA: Satyavati is right. Vyasa is her first son. Born in the mist. In a way, he's part of the family.

GANESHA: But he's the author of the poem.

BHISHMA: Precisely. It's up to him to do the necessary.

GANESHA: Speaking as the scribe, I find this totally unacceptable.

SATYAVATI: Didn't you say when you got here: I am the bringer of peace?

GANESHA: Yes, but he is dirty. Nauseating.

SATYAVATI: So much the better. If the princesses can accept his sickly smell, his muddy skin, then their children will be all the more admirable. *She comes close to Vyasa:* My son, are you in good health?

VYASA: Yes, mother, in very good health.

SATYAVATI: I am glad to hear it. *She claps her hands.* Quick! Tell the princesses a new husband has been found for them. Bathe them, perfume them, dress them in transparent silk! *While the princesses— delighted at the idea of a new husband—are being made ready, Satyavati returns to Vyasa, saying:* The destiny of a whole race is in your hands. No weakness is permitted. Stiffen your resolve, my son, let your great work proceed. *Satyavati goes up to the first princess, who is putting the final touches to her appearance.* Today, your brother-in-law will take you tenderly to his breast. Bring your family back to life and rejoice. *Satyavati and Bhishma withdraw discreetly. Vyasa goes toward the first princess, but the sight of him makes her cry with disgust. She drops to the ground, closing her eyes. Vyasa takes her, then, as he gets up, he says:*

VYASA: Why did you close your eyes? So as not to see me? Because my body is caked in mud, my beard yellow with age? *The princess does not reply.* I have given you my sperm and you will have a son. He will be called Dhritarashtra and he will be king. But as you closed your eyes on seeing me, he will be born blind.

SATYAVATI: No. A king can't be blind. *The first princess leaves; the second enters.* It's time for the second princess. Give us another son, I beg you. *The second princess now watches Vyasa's approach apprehensively. She neither cries nor closes her eyes, but shudders at his smell. She also drops to the ground. Vyasa takes her quickly and says, as he gets up:*

VYASA: Why is your color draining away? Why the chalk in your cheeks? Am I so loathsome? Is my odor so strong? *The princess, terrified, does not answer.* You too will have a son, but he will be white as milk and he will be known as Pandu the Pale. *Vyasa returns to his place. Ganesha greets him:*

GANESHA: My compliments. But didn't you say when you arrived, my poem is the story of a vast war?

VYASA: I did.

GANESHA: These children you've just created, you're going to lead them to the slaughter?

VYASA: You made me promise, Ganesha, never to pause in midstream.

GANESHA: True. As we were saying, two sons—Dhritarashtra the Blind and Pandu the Pale.

BOY: Go on with the story.

GANESHA: Quick!

VYASA: We skip twenty years.

*Ganesha draws a long line across the page, saying:*

GANESHA: Simple.

VYASA: Pandu and Dhritarashtra are now grown up.

GANESHA: Who is king?

BOY: Pandu, because his brother is blind.

*A woman enters, her eyes turned toward the sun.*

VYASA: You see this woman?

BOY: Yes.

VYASA: Her name is Kunti. She doesn't know it, but she's carrying the fate of the earth in her belly. Her children will be glorious, and without them you wouldn't be here.

GANESHA: Why's she looking so persistently at the sun?

VYASA: It's a secret.

GANESHA: What secret? Tell.

VYASA: No. It's the fundamental secret.

GANESHA: Ah . . . fundamental! Proceed.

BOY: King Pandu married Kunti? *Pandu and Kunti come together. A third woman joins them.*

VYASA: Yes, he took another wife as well, called Madri. No sooner married, Pandu went hunting. Who could have imagined that a simple hunt could seal the fate of the world? He saw two splendid gazelles copulating in a thicket. He shot them down, the male and the female. The two animals, locked together, fell to the ground and the female with her dying breath gasped out these learned words:

GAZELLE: Even devoured by lust and anger, men refrain from spilling blood. But science does not destroy fate, fate destroys science.

PANDU: What are you trying to say?

GAZELLE: How could you, Pandu, a man of superior learning, how could you kill my lover and myself?

PANDU: Men have the right to kill gazelles. Men, and especially kings. Why do you blame me?

GAZELLE: I blame you for not respecting the joys of love. You struck me down at a moment that all creatures find sweet. And you know that a woman's pleasure is superior to all other pleasures. What had I done to you? Pitiless man, I show you no pity. I curse you. You will feel the fury of a love which you cannot appease. For, if one day you take one of your wives in your arms, at that moment you will die, as I do now. *The gazelle dies. The two women run to Pandu, who lays down his arms and princely clothes, crying out:*

PANDU: I'm cursed. I must vanish without a trace in the forests. Tell Satyavati, tell Bhishma that Pandu now decrees his own everlasting exile. *He goes over to his blind brother and puts a silk scarf ceremoniously around his neck.* Dhritarashtra, my brother, you are king. *Pandu walks away. His two wives follow him.*

KUNTI: And Madri, and me? If you leave us, our lives are over.

PANDU: Let me go. I've nothing to offer you. Only poverty and the lonely road.

MADRI: We'll follow you. *Pandu leaves with his two wives.*

BOY: *To Vyasa* But you said Kunti will have glorious children. How will she manage?

VYASA: Now for the moment of truth! *A sudden thunderclap. Angry winds rise.*

GANESHA: Why this icy wind? Who invoked the thunder? *Pandu and his two wives press forward, struggling against the wind and the cold.*

VYASA: Pandu has reached the roof of the world with his two wives; the highest peak of the Himalayas, where the cold is brutal, where there's no relief from the howling storm. *Pandu stops. He is exhausted. He looks for shelter.* Constantly he mourns a life without children. He even offers Kunti to make love with another man.

PANDU: *To Kunti* Yes, with another man . . .

KUNTI: No. We want you.

MADRI: Yes, you alone.

PANDU: If I give you my love, I will die. *Suddenly Kunti says to him:*

KUNTI: Pandu, I have a confession to make. I possess a magic power, a mantra.

PANDU: Who gave it to you?

KUNTI: A saintly hermit, as a reward for serving him well. I was fourteen.

PANDU: What power does this mantra give you?

KUNTI: The power to call down a god at will.

MADRI: And . . . to have a child by him?

KUNTI: Yes.

MADRI: How can you be so sure?

KUNTI: I am sure.

PANDU: Have you ever tried it? *Kunti hesitates a little before replying.*

KUNTI: I told you, I am sure.

PANDU: Don't hesitate. Say your mantra.

KUNTI: Which god should I call down first?

PANDU: Evoke Dharma. Yes, Dharma. Beyond him all thought must stop. *Kunti says her mantra. Ganesha and Vyasa create an elaborate and ferocious ceremony. The boy is caught up in it, he becomes part of the ritual; Ganesha puts a sword in his hands. Shadowy figures appear in the background. Pandu says to Kunti:* I beseech you, give me another child. Evoke Vayu, god of the wind. *Kunti says her mantra a second time. Ganesha puts a club in the boy's hands. Kunti then says:*

KUNTI: Now I call on Indra, king of gods. *Ganesha puts a bow and arrow in the boy's hands. A flame leaps up. Madri then says to Kunti:*

MADRI: Kunti, lend me your mantra, so that I can have children too.

PANDU: Madri, evoke the Ashwins, the twin gods with golden eyes. *Madri says the mantra. A last flame burns. Five men come forward. Kunti names them:*

KUNTI: This is Yudhishthira, our first born, son of Dharma—irreproachable, flawless, Yudhishthira, born to be king. Here is Bhima, son of the wind, strong as thunder. At his birth, he fell on a rock and split it in two. Here is Arjuna, the perfect warrior, born to conquer.

MADRI: Here are our two sons, Nakula and Sahadeva, as inseparable as patience and wisdom. *Pandu looks with pride at his five children.*

PANDU: Five sons descended from the gods . . .

*Vyasa says to the boy:*

VYASA: They are the five sons of Pandu, the Pandavas. We will never leave them, as they are the heart of my poem.

BOY: Then I have the same blood. I come from the gods?

VYASA: That's what the story tells. *The five brothers withdraw, along with Kunti, Pandu, and Madri. Ganesha then asks:*

GANESHA: If I understand rightly, Dhritarashtra became king despite his blindness.

VYASA: Yes.

GANESHA: And he found a wife?

VYASA: Yes, a princess from the north called Gandhari. It's a beautiful story. Write it well.

GANESHA: Don't worry.

*A princess appears, carried high on a litter. She descends.*

VYASA: While waiting for the wedding, she lived in seclusion. Every day, her servant visited the city and described to her its thousand wonders. *The young girl-servant, who until then had been full of joy, now returns sad and agitated.*

GANDHARI: What's the matter? Why is your face so long? You usually sparkle with joy.

SERVANT: Princess . . .

GANDHARI: Tell me everything. Where did you go? What did you see?

SERVANT: I found my way into the prince's palace. . . .

GANDHARI: And?

SERVANT: I saw . . . I saw Dhritarashtra, your future husband.

GANDHARI: You saw him?

SERVANT: Yes.

GANDHARI: Make me see him. Is he handsome? Strong?

SERVANT: Yes, he's strong. Very strong.

GANDHARI: Then why are you crying? Answer me.

SERVANT: Princess, you have been betrayed. Dhritarashtra is blind.

GANDHARI: What do you mean?

SERVANT: Born blind.

GANDHARI: That's impossible. A king cannot be blind. You must be mistaken.

SERVANT: I asked an old guard. Dhritarashtra is blind. His eyes are dead.

GANDHARI: And they've hidden it from me? My wedding's prepared, it's announced. My hollow-eyed husband taps his way toward me in the dark, someone leads him by the hand. . . . No, it's not possible, they lied to you. If he's blind he could only reign over the night, over monsters that thrive on darkness, amidst the desperate cries of a diseased people, people who are no longer people. . . .

SERVANT: He's blind. I've seen him. *For a moment Gandhari stays motionless.*

GANDHARI: What's the use of my paint, of my dresses, if my husband will never see me? Why my hair? Why my red lips? Why my flesh? And my eyes? Give me my veil. *The servant hands a veil to Gandhari who suddenly is very calm.*

SERVANT: What are you looking at?

GANDHARI: At you. You are my last image in this world.

SERVANT: What are you doing? *Gandhari ties the band over her eyes.*

GANDHARI: I'm putting a band on my eyes. I'm tying it firmly. I will never take it off. Give me your hand, lead me to my husband. Now I can never reproach him his misfortune. *The servant takes Gandhari by the hand. At this moment Dhritarashtra, the blind king, enters. Music plays. Gandhari goes to join her husband. He passes his hand over Gandhari's face, touches the blindfold. Deeply moved, he takes her in his arms. They move away together. Gandhari disappears for a moment behind a curtain held by Vyasa and the boy.*

VYASA: When Gandhari was pregnant, she bore her fruit for two years. Nothing stirred. Her belly was heavy, very hard. *Gandhari reappears holding her enormous belly with two hands. The servant rushes up to her.*

SERVANT: Gandhari, Kunti has just given birth to a son. He is called Yudhishthira. The people say he will be king. *Gandhari stays silent for a moment, then she says to the servant:*

GANDHARI: Get an iron bar.

SERVANT: What?

GANDHARI: Obey me. Get an iron bar. *The servant takes an iron bar.* Strike me on the belly. Hard! *The servant hesitates.* Do what I tell you. Hit very hard! Strike! *The servant hits Gandhari with the iron bar.* Harder! Harder, I tell you. *The servant hits harder.* Harder still! Go on, strike! Yes. Again. I'm in labor. You're delivering me, strike! *Gandhari shouts out. The servant stops hitting her.*

BOY: Is that how babies are born?

GANESHA: Not necessarily.

*A large ball appears between the queen's legs.*

GANDHARI: What has just come out of my womb?

SERVANT: A ball of flesh. Like metal.

GANDHARI: It's crying? It moves?

SERVANT: No, it's cold and hard.

GANDHARI: Throw the ball into a well and leave me alone. *The servant takes the ball but Vyasa intervenes:*

VYASA: No. Throw nothing away. Cut the ball into a hundred pieces, put them into a hundred earthenware jars. Sprinkle them with fresh water. Out of them will come a hundred sons. *The servant goes out taking the ball with her.*

BOY: A hundred sons?

VYASA: The first one burst into life with the blood-curdling bray of an anguished ass. He was called Duryodhana, the Hard to Conquer. Remember that name.

GANESHA: Duryodhana.

*Frightful noises are heard as though to greet the birth of Duryodhana who rolls on the ground screaming. Dhritarashtra, the blind emperor, reappears, still guided by Bhishma.*

DHRITARASHTRA: Bhishma, what are these sounds?

BHISHMA: Winds, carnivorous animals, angry birds of prey, and the screams of your son.

DHRITARASHTRA: The air is thick. It crushes me. I can't breathe. How is the sky?

BHISHMA: On fire.

DHRITARASHTRA: You, who have seen so much, tell me. What do these omens mean?

BHISHMA: They all point toward your son. They say, Duryodhana comes to destroy. If you wish to preserve your race, sacrifice him. *Dhristarashtra and Gandhari catch hold of their son, who goes on screaming.*

DHRITARASHTRA: My newborn son? Sacrifice him?

BHISHMA: That's what I hear.

DHRITARASHTRA: You've never held a child in your arms. You don't know what it means to say, "I'll shed my own blood." Bhishma, I can't kill my son.

GANDHARI: Even if he howls, even if he brings with him hatred and terror, no one will kill my first-born child without killing me myself. *They withdraw. The chilling noises have stopped. All becomes peaceful and luminous. Madri, almost naked, is now in a wood near a river. Pandu reappears and goes over to Madri.*

PANDU: Madri, hear how the forest whispers and sings. Can you taste the honey in the breeze? The birds chuckle, the insects tremble with joy, the flowers open, it's the first day of spring and the sun streams through your dress. . . .

MADRI: Pandu, don't touch me. If you love me, you die.

PANDU: I know, but when I look at you, I prefer love to life. Not a word. *He wants to take her, she resists.*

MADRI: Don't tempt death. Death is seducing you. Keep away.

PANDU: There's no risk for you, no danger. Lie down in the grass.

MADRI: No. You'll need to take me by force. *As Pandu penetrates her, he cries out and dies. Madri leaps to her feet, calling:* Kunti! Kunti! Come! Without the children. *Kunti runs on and sees the king's lifeless body.* Kunti, Pandu died while trying to love me.

KUNTI: But weren't you there to watch over him? How could you let him stir, grow hard, here, in this lonely place? How could he forget the curse? What have you done?

MADRI: I wanted to save him but his destiny carried him away.

KUNTI: Ah, you are happier than I am, because you have seen his face glow with desire. I will follow him to the other shore.

MADRI: No, as it's in my arms that he breathed his last breath, it is I who will die. I will go to the land of death to calm his passion. I give you my sons, who no longer have a father in this world.

KUNTI: They will be like my sons, they will share everything.

MADRI: Burn my body along with the king. Come. Help me to die. *The two women disappear. A pyre is lit. Satyavati goes up to Vyasa.*

SATYAVATI: Vyasa, my son. Madri has thrown herself into the fire in front of all the people. I am old, my heart is choked with ashes, and I ask myself: why this death?

VYASA: Because the earth has lost its youth, which has gone by like a happy dream. Now, each day brings us closer to barrenness, to destruction.

SATYAVATI: What is this terrible struggle you foresee?

VYASA: A universal struggle without pity, an outrage to intelligent man. The heroes will perish without knowing why.

SATYAVATI: Who will be the winner?

VYASA: I don't know, for all depends on the hearts of men and there I can't see clearly.

SATYAVATI: Can I help you?

VYASA: You have helped me enough, mother. Go far away, into the forest, disappear among the trees.

SATYAVATI: And you. You will go on?

VYASA: To the very end. *Satyavati leaves.*

# YOUTH

*As Satyvati disappears, Vyasa asks Ganesha:*

VYASA: Ganesha, you're writing everything?

GANESHA: I'm writing everything and I understand everything.

VYASA: Now we skip . . .

GANESHA: Twenty years?

VYASA: Twenty years.

GANESHA: So your heroes are now twenty.

VYASA: Exactly. *Bhima appears at this moment.*

GANESHA: Who's this?

BOY: Bhima, the strongest man in the world. *Bhima, who suddenly seems in pain, falls to the ground as though dead. Dushassana, one of Duryodhana's brothers, appears and calls:*

DUSHASSANA: Duryodhana! My brother! *Duryodhana rushes in.*

DURYODHANA: Yes, I'm here. What are you doing?

DUSHASSANA: Look at Bhima!

DURYODHANA: He's dead?

DUSHASSANA: He doesn't move. *They go up to Bhima's body very prudently as the boy asks:*

BOY: Who's with Duryodhana?

VYASA: Dushassana, the most dangerous of the hundred brothers. *Dushassana talks to Bhima's inanimate body:*

DUSHASSANA: Bhima, big beast, wolf-belly, give you food and drink and it's gobble, gobble . . .

DURYODHANA: Watch out, Dushassana.

DUSHASSANA: I slipped a poison into your wine and you gulped down your death. *Suddenly, as the brothers are leaning over him, Bhima grabs them savagely by the throat. They try to get away.* No, don't kill me!

BHIMA: You wanted to kill me. You said so yourself . . . but a snake bit me and its venom saved my life.

DURYODHANA: Let go! Bhishma! Quick! Help us. *Yudhishthira enters with Arjuna and orders:*

YUDHISHTHIRA: Bhima! Take your hands away!

ARJUNA: Let them go!

BHIMA: I'll only let them go dead. I'm cleaning up the earth. *No one can make Bhima release them. Duryodhana and Dushassana are almost suffocated.*
    *At this moment a man appears. He is about fifty, poorly dressed, and carrying a light bag. He goes up to Bhima and takes his wrist. Bhima screams, doubling up with pain. He lets the two brothers go and wants to hit the unknown person, who makes some lightning moves. Bhima collapses on the ground. Humiliated, he gets to his feet again. Then, with a great roar he leaves and comes back immediately, brandishing a tree that he has just pulled out of the ground.*

YUDHISHTHIRA: Bhima! Put down that tree!

BHIMA: No.

ARJUNA: Look out! *Bhima rushes forward. Everyone moves away except the older man, who awaits Bhima calmly. Just as Bhima tries to hit him with the tree, he moves away, the tree falls to the ground and Bhima is as though paralyzed, then thrown to the ground by a single flash of the newcomer's stick. Yudhishthira then asks:*

YUDHISHTHIRA: Who are you?

DRONA: I'm the new teacher.

ARJUNA: What's your name?

YUDHISHTHIRA: Who has sent you?

DRONA: My name is Drona. No one has sent me. I'm here for your education. *Bhishma appears and goes up to Drona. He seems happy to see him.*

BHISHMA: Are you really Drona?

DRONA: Yes.

BHISHMA: I've heard much of you. They say that amongst the wise you are the wisest, and among masters of arms you are supreme.

DRONA: Bhishma! *They greet each other warmly.*

BHISHMA: Is it true that you have mastered all the possible forms of war?

DRONA: As well as you, Bhishma.

BHISHMA: And you also know sacred weapons that even the gods hold secret?

DRONA: Yes, I know them too.

BHISHMA: I am happy you have come to our city. These are the sons of Pandu and the sons of Dhritarashtra, the Pandavas and the Kauravas. At the death of Pandu, I decided to raise them together, but since childhood everything tears them apart.

DRONA: So I see.

ARJUNA: Duryodhana and all his brothers want to kill us.

DURYODHANA: No! Bhima hits first. He tries to strangle us. Day after day.

BHIMA: Duryodhana is panting with greed. He wants the kingdom. He wants to destroy us.

BHISHMA: Silence! *The two groups of cousins who, once again, had almost come to blows, are quiet. Bhishma asks Drona:* When do you begin?

DRONA: I've begun. *Drona gives a brief order. They all take their bows. Then Drona raises a hand and says:* On top of this tree I've placed a vulture made of straw and rags. Yudhishthira, take your bow. Aim. *Yudhishthira obeys.* What do you see?

YUDHISHTHIRA: I see the vulture.

DRONA: Do you see the tree?

YUDHISHTHIRA: Yes, I see the tree. I see the bow and the arrow, I see my arm, I see my brothers, and I see you.

DRONA: Back to your place. Nakula, come here. You too, Bhima. You too, Duryodhana. Aim at the bird. What do you see? *They bend their bows and take aim.*

NAKULA: I see the bird, the sky . . .

BHIMA: . . . the branches of the tree, my hand . . .

DRONA: Do you see your brothers?

BHIMA: Yes, I see them.

DURYODHANA: I see the bird, I see my bow, I see the top of the tree.

BHIMA: I see a cloud in the sky.

DRONA: Back. All of you. Useless to shoot. Arjuna, take your bow. Aim. *Arjuna obeys. Once in position, not a muscle moves.* What do you see?

ARJUNA: A vulture.

DRONA: Describe the vulture.

ARJUNA: I can't.

DRONA: Why?

ARJUNA: I can only see its head.

DRONA: Release your arrow. *Arjuna shoots and the bird falls, pierced through by the arrow. Drona takes Arjuna's hands and says to him:* I'll make you the finest archer in the world.

ARJUNA: You'll teach me everything?

DRONA: Yes, everything.

ARJUNA: Even sacred weapons?

DRONA: No. I keep for myself the secret of sacred weapons. They must never be launched against men.

ARJUNA: Why have weapons if you cannot make use of them?

DRONA: Because even their dimmest glow could shrivel up the earth. Arjuna, none of my pupils will be your equal. But I need you to make a promise: if, one day, destiny places us face to face, if you see me advancing menacingly toward you, you must fight me and you must fight to kill. *Arjuna is silent a moment before saying:*

ARJUNA: Yes, I promise. *Arjuna is about to withdraw when a young man comes running in, throwing himself at Drona's feet and saying:*

EKALAVYA: Drona, you are my master, I know it. My name is Ekalavya. I come from the other side of the world to receive your teaching. Take me in your school.

DRONA: No.

EKALAVYA: Why? Like you, Drona, I can give up riches and pleasure. I only wish to learn.

DRONA: No. I've enough pupils. Go away. *Vyasa takes up the story, telling the boy:*

VYASA: Thus rejected, the adolescent withdrew to the depths of a wood and there, alone, he carved in stone the living likeness of Drona. Each day, devoutly, he worshipped this idol and trained himself under its gaze. *Drona, suddenly motionless, becomes the statue in front of which Ekalavya does his exercises.* Watched over by the statue, he acquired the most astonishing skills. He even managed to plant seven arrows in the jaws of a dog in the space of a single bark. *Arjuna reappears and immediately Drona is himself once more, as though in his own dwelling.*

ARJUNA: Drona, you haven't kept your promise.

DRONA: In what way?

ARJUNA: You promised I'd be the best. None of your pupils would be my rival. Ekalavya has planted seven arrows in the jaws of a barking dog, and Ekalavya says he's your pupil.

DRONA: Come! *Drona, accompanied by Arjuna goes into the forest. Here, the young man is practicing with a sword. Seeing Drona, he is surprised and delighted, and throws himself down on the ground.*

EKALAVYA: Master, I kiss the earth before you. I am your pupil. Your visit brings me unexpected joy.

DRONA: If you are my pupil, you must pay me for my lessons.

EKALAVYA: Ask what you wish. I owe you everything.

DRONA: Give me the thumb of your right hand.

EKALAVYA: Here it is. *Ekalavya takes his sword, cuts off his thumb and gives it to Drona who leaves at once.*

BOY: He cut off his thumb?

ARJUNA: Smiling. Without hesitation.

BOY: And he lost his skill?

ARJUNA: Yes, his skill and his strength.

BOY: And you are satisfied with such an act of cruelty?

ARJUNA: It's not cruelty. It's foresight. *The stage lights go out except for one lamp. Arjuna is seated, alone. He is eating by the light of the lamp.*

VYASA: *To the boy* Watch closely. *Vyasa puts out the light. Arjuna continues his meal in the dark. Suddenly he stops and says:*

ARJUNA: The wind has put out my lamp. I see nothing. But nonetheless my hand finds its way to my mouth. Why not aim my arrows the same way, why not shoot in the dark? *Arjuna puts down his bowl and starts to shoot in the dark. The light returns. Arjuna has not stopped shooting. The place has changed. The court is gathered for a tournament and Arjuna is performing an extraordinary series of feats.*

DRONA: He's incomparable. Even his thoughts are arrows. *Dhritarashtra and Gandhari are there. Bhishma tells them what is happening. Dushassana, Duryodhana, the other Pandavas, Drona, and Kunti are all present. Each of Arjuna's feats is applauded.*

DHRITARASHTRA: How I envy those who have eyes! *Then a voice calls:*

KARNA: Son of Kunti! *All are silent. An armed man appears.*

GANDHARI: Who is that?

BHISHMA: A stranger.

DHRITARASHTRA: Who is he?

BHISHMA: I've never seen him before. *The man stops in front of Arjuna and says to him:*

KARNA: Son of Kunti, I can do all that you have done as well as you—even better. Watch. *The newcomer shoots toward the sky. A bird falls, pierced by the arrow. The feat is greeted by murmurs as, without even looking at the bird, the newcomer says:* I hit him in the left eye. *Duryodhana snatches up the bird and brandishes it.*

DURYODHANA: What's your name?

KARNA: Karna.

DURYODHANA: Welcome. Come into my arms. *The two men embrace. Arjuna addresses Karna:*

ARJUNA: You are here, but you haven't been invited. You speak but you have not been addressed.

KARNA: Isn't this place of arms open to all? Prepare yourself, Arjuna, we are going to fight. *The two men prepare to fight. Kunti throws herself at Dhritarashtra's feet.*

KUNTI: Dhritarashtra, listen to me!

DHRITARASHTRA: Who are you? What do you want?

KUNTI: I am Kunti. Keep them apart. Prevent them from fighting.

DHRITARASHTRA: For what reason?

KUNTI: They're driven by hate. They will kill one another. I know it.

DHRITARASHTRA: What's the reason for this hatred?

KUNTI: Dhritarashtra, I implore you, don't allow them to fight, don't. . . . *Kunti swoons at the king's feet.*

BHISHMA: She's fainted.

GANDHARI: Kunti's fainted?

GANESHA: Vyasa, I don't understand what's going on. As a result, my hand is frozen.

VYASA: I stop all motion. *Everyone remains motionless, heads bowed, as Kunti slowly gets up.* You remember Kunti's mantra, her magic power?

BOY: Yes.

VYASA: From the age of fifteen, before her marriage with Pandu, Kunti had already made use of it in secret.

BOY: With whom?

VYASA: With the sun.

GANESHA: Ah, the fundamental secret.

VYASA: Yes, she invoked the sun and at once the sun appeared. *Kunti mouths several short words. Immediately the sun appears in all its glory.*

SUN: I am here, Kunti. I am the sun. You conjured me and I have come. What is your wish, young lady?

KUNTI: Oh, excuse me. I wanted to try out a mantra, that's all.

SUN: Ah, no, Kunti, it's not all. You can't have brought me down just for that. It's unthinkable. You must come into my arms and I'll give you a son.

KUNTI: A son! I can't, I'm a virgin, I am only fifteen. You must always protect women, even when they're guilty.

SUN: I know all that, but one doesn't disturb the sun for nothing.

KUNTI: Go back to the sky. Forget what I did. I'm only a child. Forgive me.

SUN: I'll say it again: it's impossible. The sun is going to be your lover, the sun will give you a son, and I can reassure you, your virginity will remain intact. Abandon all your fears and come into my arms. *Kunti allows herself to be loved by the sun.*

VYASA: Instantly they had a son, a radiant son, wearing a golden breastplate. But Kunti was afraid. She hid her fault, she put the child in a basket and left him to a river's whim. He survived, a chariot driver found him and brought him up.

*The boy points to Karna and says:*

BOY: It's him? It's Karna?

VYASA: Yes, it's him.

BOY: We must stop him fighting against his brother!

VYASA: No, I forbid it. *Karna straightens himself. Kunti has left. The inanimate figures move again.*

KARNA: Arjuna, wherever you look, I'll always be ahead. Why are you waiting? Take up your arms. I am ready. *Duryodhana gives Arjuna his sword. Karna and Arjuna prepare to fight. Then Drona says to Karna:*

DRONA: Arjuna comes from a Kshatriya family, he is of royal birth and cannot fight an inferior person. Tell us your father's name. *Karna is silent for a moment.* At least tell us your mother's name and I will let you fight. *Karna lowers his head without replying.* You lower your head. You don't reply.

GANDHARI: Karna, are you ashamed of your mother, or don't you know her?

KARNA: I don't know her.

ARJUNA: *To Karna* Withdraw. This is not your place. *Karna withdraws. Arjuna tries to return Duryodhana's sword, but Duryodhana calls Karna back.*

DURYODHANA: Karna. If you have to be a prince to fight, I consecrate you here. Come. I give you the land of Anga. I name you king. *He places his hand on Karna's head, his father nodding his consent. After an astonished silence, Karna says to him:*

KARNA: What can I give you in exchange?

DURYODHANA: Your friendship.

KARNA: It's yours. Forever true. *The two men embrace, then Duryodhana declares:*

DURYODHANA: Now the fight can begin. *But suddenly an old man in poor rough clothes comes in, very intimidated. He grasps Karna and says:*

ADHIRATHA: Karna, I've been searching for you. Karna . . . I was worried.

*Drona asks the new arrival:*

DRONA: Who are you?

ADHIRATHA: I'm a driver. My name is Adhiratha. I'm looking for my son Karna.

DRONA: *To Karna* He's your father?

KARNA: Yes, my father.

BHIMA: The son of a driver! Give him a whip and a shovel for the dung! And harness asses to his wagon!

DURYODHANA: Bhima, quiet! Or I'll cut out your tongue! *Bhima goes on jeering:*

BHIMA: They've set a driver's son on the throne of Anga! *Duryodhana throws himself at Bhima, knocks him down. He, in turn, is checked by Drona. Gradually Duryodhana grows calmer and he says to Bhima:*

DURYODHANA: Shut your mouth and don't speak of birth. Birth is obscure and men are like rivers whose origins are often unknown. I look at Karna and I'm not mistaken. I see his power edged with mystery and he'll forever be my friend. The setting sun seems to whisper it's true. Come, Karna, the day is over. *Duryodhana takes his sword from Arjuna's hands. Karna says to Arjuna:*

KARNA: Arjuna, you have rejected me. Inevitably, one day we will fight and I will kill you. *Karna and Duryodhana leave together. Gandhari, and Dhritarashtra guided by Bhishma, follow them. As Drona passes in front of him, Yudhishthira says:*

YUDHISHTHIRA: That man has taught me fear. I feel deep down that Karna is irresistible. What do you think?

DRONA: Only destiny is irresistible. *They all leave.*

# MARRIAGE AND KINGDOM

*Arjuna comes in full of joy and joins his mother and brothers. He addresses Kunti, who has her back turned. She is with his brothers.*

ARJUNA: Mother, guess what I've won! *Kunti replies without turning around:*

KUNTI: You must share everything with your brothers.

ARJUNA: But it's a woman! *Kunti turns and sees Arjuna. Holding herself modestly in the distance is a veiled woman.* I won her in a tournament, far from here. All the princes of the world wanted her. But I won. And she chose me.

KUNTI: What did I say?

ARJUNA: You said, "You must share everything with your brothers."

KUNTI: I can't take back my word. You must do as I say.

BOY: Why?

*It is Vyasa that replies:*

VYASA: Because an untruth can never cross her lips. What Kunti says is true. *Kunti looks at the newcomer and asks:*

KUNTI: What is her name?

ARJUNA: Draupadi. She's the paragon of women.

KUNTI: You must do what I said. You must share Draupadi among you, but she mustn't suffer in any way. *For a moment they ponder on this. Vyasa says to the boy:*

VYASA: Watch closely what happens next—for the first time in the history of the world.

YUDHISHTHIRA: There is only one question: do we all love Draupadi?

BHIMA: Yes, I already feel I love her.

ARJUNA: I love her deeply.

NAKULA: So do I.

SAHADEVA: So do I.

YUDHISHTHIRA: Yes, I love her too. All of a sudden love has appeared among us, like a light. As our mother cannot tell a lie, as we all love Draupadi, we will have to marry her, all five of us.

KUNTI: Yes, this is how it should be. Draupadi will have five husbands.

BHIMA: Her father won't be outraged?

KUNTI: You must tell him that nothing must ever come between you.

NAKULA: But if Draupadi comes between us? If she likes one of us more than another? If there's one she despises? If jealousy tears us apart?

KUNTI: What I've said is said. Destiny slipped into my words without warning. She must be your wife and she can be. For this first night, may a common sleep unite us. Protect her well.

*The five Pandavas, Draupadi, and Kunti make ready for the first night. The five brothers lie down side by side and Draupadi lays herself at their feet. Kunti goes to sleep too—on the other side. It is night. The boy approaches the sleepers and asks:*

BOY: Vyasa, why did my family murder one another?

VYASA: Because they forgot the essential.

BOY: And nothing could save them?

VYASA: Listen. *A flute is heard.* A flute draws near.

BOY: Yes.

VYASA: Krishna is going to make his entrance.

BOY: Krishna?

VYASA: Krishna himself.

BOY: Krishna is going to play a part in your story!

VYASA: He's going to play, as always, the leading role.

GANESHA: Listen to me. *The boy listens to the night. The flute can be heard in the distance. The Pandavas, their wife, and their mother all sleep deeply.* The worlds swarm with an infinity of creatures, those we see, those we never see; Naga snakes who live in the depths of the earth or in vast palaces on the sea's bed; Rakshasas, monsters of the forest's night who live off human flesh; Gandharvas, frail creatures who glide between us and the sky; Apsarasas, Danavas, Yakshas and the long glittering chain of gods who live like all beings in the shadow of death. Three gods rule the universe, three who are also one: Brahma, the creator—we can never see him, but we are told he sleeps on the limitless ocean; Shiva, the destroyer, the burning Shiva always present when history ends—always there when he's least expected. The third is Vishnu who is quite the reverse. It is he who maintains the worlds, it is he who makes them endure. When chaos threatens, as it does now, Vishnu takes on a human form and descends among us to play his role. Some hint that he might have come down as Krishna.

BOY: Is it true?

GANESHA: One can never be sure. But you've heard of his extraordinary feats?

BOY: Yes.

GANESHA: Of his sixteen thousand wives? Of his countless children?

Boy: Of the mountain he held on one finger?

Ganesha: Of the terrifying disc which comes when he calls it and which can destroy everything?

Boy: I'm going to see Krishna? It's his flute I hear? He's on his way?

Ganesha: Perhaps he's already here.

Boy: In what form?

Ganesha: In the form of a man, because he is a man. Watch carefully. His action is subtle, mysteriously clear. At the same instant, they say, he can be everywhere—here, there—he is water and the trembling of a leaf, he's you, he's fire, he's the heart of all that's invisible.

Boy: He's you as well?

Ganesha: Naturally. *Ganesha removes his elephant's head and disappears for a moment behind a curtain held by Vyasa and the boy. When they lift the curtain, he is Krishna, asleep. Everything is flooded with light. The Pandavas, Draupadi, and Kunti wake and greet Krishna, their friend.*

Yudhishthira: Krishna, why have you sent for us?

Krishna: I heard the earth complain.

Yudhishthira: What did she say?

Krishna: She said: "Men have become arrogant. Every day they give me fresh wounds. There are more and more of them, ever more violent, driven by thoughts of conquest. Foolish men trample me. I shudder and I ask myself: 'What will they do next?' "

*A moment's silence.*

Yudhishthira: What can save the earth?

Krishna: I sent men with huge ears into the crowd. This is what they say: "The people want a king who will be calm and just, *(Looking at Yudhishthira)* a legitimate king." And the earth added: "I want this king. I insist on him. Without him, I am lost."

YUDHISHTHIRA: Am I this king?

KRISHNA: Who else?

YUDHISHTHIRA: Krishna, what must I do now?

KRISHNA: All night the blind king thinks of you. A decision must be made, the time has come, he knows it. He knows that all living creatures call for you. That you are the only true king. But his heart is racked with uncertainty. He loves his invisible kingdom and he is besotted with his son. *Yudhishthira rises and says to his brothers:*

YUDHISHTHIRA: Our youth is over. We will go to the king. *They leave. At the last moment Krishna holds Arjuna back.*

KRISHNA: Arjuna. *Arjuna sits down next to Krishna.* You are uneasy.

ARJUNA: The sun is scorching the earth, the heat is unusual; at night the animals make human cries. Krishna, there's something I must ask you.

*A young woman (Subhadra) appears. She offers a tray with a drink and fruits to Arjuna, saying to him:*

SUBHADRA: This is to quench your thirst. *Arjuna takes the tray and his gaze follows the young woman as she moves away. He asks her:*

ARJUNA: Who are you?

KRISHNA: She is Subhadra, my sister. She left this ring for you. I think she loves you. *Krishna takes a ring from the tray and shows it to Arjuna who takes it.*

ARJUNA: Can I stay a few days with you?

KRISHNA: Abandoning your brother just when his life becomes real? *Arjuna does not reply.* Sometimes you frighten me. At any moment your family, your friends, the entire earth may need you.

ARJUNA: Yes, enemies are evolving all around us, in the shadows. I can't forget them, not for an instant. But how can one ignore a woman's smile when it beckons to you? *Krishna remains silent. Subhadra withdraws.* If war rumbles in the distance like a storm that never breaks, must I waste all my life preparing for it and die thwarted and useless?

KRISHNA: Arjuna, I tell you with absolute conviction, you won't have a choice between peace and war.

ARJUNA: What will be my choice?

KRISHNA: Between a war and another war.

ARJUNA: The other war—where will it take place? On a battlefield or in my heart?

KRISHNA: I don't see a real difference. Go back to your family. *Arjuna rises.* Don't forget to greet my sister Subhadra before you leave. *Arjuna prepares to leave.* Arjuna! Wasn't there something you wanted to ask me?

ARJUNA: You've answered me. *The two men leave.*

    *The blind king enters, alone and pensive. A moment later Duryodhana enters, accompanied by Dushassana and Karna.*

DURYODHANA: Why did you agree to see them? Do you want to give them a land of their own? Cut into pieces what should remain one? Why treat the Pandavas as your sons when they are our enemies? Our natural enemies.

DHRITARASHTRA: I am guided by Bhishma. *Duryodhana turns to Bhishma, who has just come in with Gandhari and Drona.*

DURYODHANA: Bhishma has always been on their side. But how could you have noticed it, you who see nothing? *Dhritarashtra tries to hit his son who dodges.*

DHRITARASHTRA: What should I do? Tell me.

BHISHMA: Regain your calm.

DRONA: They are here.

*The five Pandavas, accompanied by Krishna, enter and take their places.*

DHRITARASHTRA: My sons—for you are my sons—are you there?

YUDHISHTHIRA: We are here before you.

DHRITARASHTRA: Greetings, Krishna. I know you come with them.

KRISHNA: Greetings. What have you decided?

DHRITARASHTRA: So that peace can always shine on our family, I am giving away part of my kingdom.

ARJUNA: What lands are you giving us?

DHRITARASHTRA: I'm giving you the land of Khandava–Prastha.

BHIMA: What! Those stinking bogs! Those gruesome forests!

YUDHISHTHIRA: Silence, Bhima. *To Dhritarashtra* I accept and I thank you.

BHIMA: Why take charity like a beggar? Yudhishthira, what demon has invaded your mind? *He rips up a nearby tree and brandishes it threateningly. He is beside himself. Duryodhana, Dushassana, and Karna are immediately on their guard. Yudhishthira tries to calm Bhima. Drona protects the king.*

YUDHISHTHIRA: Put that down.

BHIMA: No.

YUDHISHTHIRA: Put that back in its place and calm down.

BHIMA: Why grovel at their feet? They've only one thought, throw us out of the kingdom where our rights are as good as theirs. And you, you say, "Thank you, I touch your feet, I'm most grateful." What do you put above justice? Above our destiny? What?

YUDHISHTHIRA: Put that tree back where you took it from. *Unwillingly, Bhima lowers the tree but keeps it on his shoulder. Bhishma goes up to Yudhishthira and says to him:*

BHISHMA: Go, dry up the marshes. Plough the harsh earth that awaits you, dig out lakes that reflect the sky, build a dazzling city and draw the universe to it.

YUDHISHTHIRA: We take our leave. *Krishna and the Pandavas withdraw. Duryodhana then says to Dhritarashtra:*

DURYODHANA: Father, you thought you had made peace. You have launched a war. Bhima will never let us go.

DUSHASSANA: We must surprise Bhima and destroy him. We must separate them from Krishna by cunning. They have one wife for five, call in experts in erotics and ask them how to sow jealousy.

*Karna intervenes to say to Dushassana:*

KARNA: Don't despise them. We are what we are because pleasures and sorrows were inscribed in our blood long ago. Our will comes from far. Nothing can separate them from Krishna, no amount of cunning can bring them down. *And to Duryodhana:* If you want to destroy them—I've always said so—attack them head-on. *Karna draws Duryodhana along by the arm, still talking:* I'm your friend. Why are you afraid? *They leave. Dushassana follows them. Dhritarashtra then asks Bhishma:*

DHRITARASHTRA: Bhishma, have I done well?

BHISHMA: Yes.

DHRITARASHTRA: The sons of my brother Pandu are my sons.

GANDHARI: But in your heart you have a secret preference.

DHRITARASHTRA: So have you, Gandhari.

GANDHARI: And when one prefers one's own children to the children of others, war is near. *They go to leave. Dhritarashtra asks again:*

DHRITARASHTRA: Bhishma, in the event of war, which side will you take?

BHISHMA: I will, unfortunately, be loyal to you.

DHRITARASHTRA: And you, Drona?

DRONA: I'm at your service. *They all leave.*
   *In the half-dark, a strange figure (Maya) enters, calling:*

MAYA: Yudhishthira! I'm looking for Yudhishthira! Where is he?

YUDHISHTHIRA: I am here. Who are you?

MAYA: You don't know me?

YUDHISHTHIRA: No.

MAYA: All educated people know me. I am Maya, the supreme architect. Maya, master of every illusion. I wish to accomplish a marvel for you. I want to build you a palace.

YUDHISHTHIRA: What sort of palace?

MAYA: Listen . . . my invisible workers, Rakshasas who fly through the air, are already at work. It will be a palace unequaled in the three worlds. A magic palace, where thoughts become real.

YUDHISHTHIRA: Where thoughts become real.

MAYA: Yes.

YUDHISHTHIRA: When will it be ready?

MAYA: It is ready. *In fact the palace has appeared.*

YUDHISHTHIRA: Stay with us.

MAYA: I can't. I have to build a bridge.

YUDHISHTHIRA: Over which river?

MAYA: The ocean. *Maya vanishes.*

# THE KING OF KINGS

*A picture of happiness.*

*Several years have passed. The five Pandavas are in their palace with Draupadi and Subhadra, who is sitting close to Arjuna, a baby in her arms. They are peacefully eating fruit and drinking while listening to music. They welcome Krishna who is coming to visit them, saying as he enters:*

KRISHNA: Greetings, Yudhishthira, greetings to you all. Coming here, I looked at the landscape with admiration and I said to myself: "They have made the desert bloom, a deep fleece of wheat clothes the fields." Is it true that a good king brings rain? That he chases away disease?

YUDHISHTHIRA: I live in peace with my brothers. By her simple presence, Draupadi binds us together. She has given us each a son. *Krishna greets Subhadra and looks at the baby in her arms:*

KRISHNA: I greet you, Subhadra.

SUBHADRA: I greet you, my brother.

KRISHNA: You seem well and happy.

SUBHADRA: It's true. I've found my family.

KRISHNA: And this is my nephew, the young Abhimanyu. Arjuna, your son is a jewel. Draupadi, my devoted greetings. How do you get on with this new wife?

DRAUPADI: I love her like a younger sister.

KRISHNA: That's rare and beautiful. As I arrived, I caught sight of Vyasa. *Yudhishthira seems worried at this and asks:*

YUDHISHTHIRA: What does he want?

KRISHNA: Ask him. *Vyasa has just appeared with the boy.*

YUDHISHTHIRA: Vyasa, you are still there?

VYASA: Yes.

YUDHISHTHIRA: You haven't finished your poem?

VYASA: You imagined it finished?

YUDHISHTHIRA: We live in harmony. The poor are fed. Each man helps his neighbor. Life is calm, death is peaceful. What more can you want from a poem?

VYASA: You can't stop halfway up the mountain.

YUDHISHTHIRA: What's my destination?

VYASA: You must celebrate the great sacrifice and be crowned king of kings.

YUDHISHTHIRA: No. I don't want that title. When I hear it, my heart goes dry, all joy fades. Why ask other kings to pay me homage?

VYASA: The request comes from the kings themselves. They say: "The golden age has reappeared on earth! Yudhishthira is the best of kings. Let him be our king."

YUDHISHTHIRA: I am too unprepared. I have no desire for the crown.

VYASA: Don't deceive yourself. All creatures love you, you have pondered deeply, you are the son of Dharma.

ARJUNA: And your brothers are your body. Bhima is your neck and shoulders, Nakula and Sahadeva are your arms and legs, I am your eyes and your hand.

YUDHISHTHIRA: What do you say, Krishna?

KRISHNA: For many, you are the only defense against all these dangers.

YUDHISHTHIRA: What dangers? Do you see them clearly?

KRISHNA: Destruction never approaches weapon in hand. It comes slyly on tiptoe, making you see bad in good and good in bad.

YUDHISHTHIRA: Now, suddenly, all I want is to withdraw to the woods and live off nothing.

VYASA: If you withdraw, another king will take your place, because there's a horde of pretenders.

KRISHNA: But none is ruler of himself, except you.

YUDHISHTHIRA: If I accept this title, my uncle and my cousins will feel threatened, they will plunge us into war. *To Krishna* How can you call me a legitimate king if I condemn the earth to a horrifying death?

ARJUNA: Dhritarashtra calls us his sons. He will be proud to see one of his sons on the highest throne.

KRISHNA: Invite him to your coronation.

VYASA: Decide.

KRISHNA: Resist what resists in you. Become yourself. *Yudhishthira ponders for a moment. Everyone respects his silence and awaits his decision. Then he speaks:*

YUDHISHTHIRA: Yes, let them come! Let them all come! Let them bring the fruits of the earth to the sacrifice! Invite all the kings; treat them better than brothers! *Music plays, the kings arrive. Yudhishthira greets them:* Bhishma, thank you for your presence. Drona, Karna, stay close to me today. *Duryodhana is the last to appear.* Duryodhana, thank you for being with me. You are especially welcome. *They all take their places. Yudhishthira asks Bhishma:* Bhishma, to whom should I propose the place of honor?

BHISHMA: Offer it to Krishna. He is the light of this assembly.

*At this point, a young king (Sisupala), who has not yet taken his place like the others, asks:*

SISUPALA: Why always give the place of honor to Krishna?

YUDHISHTHIRA: Sisupala, take your seat. *But Sisupala continues, gradually raising his tone:*

SISUPALA: Bhishma, do you only wish to please? To flatter? Krishna is not the oldest, nor the strongest. How can you compare him with Dhritarashtra, with Duryodhana? Or Jayadratha, or Satyaki? You're in the presence of Drona, of Karna—how can you put him above them? How can you, Bhishma, put Krishna above yourself? *Everyone is silent.* I am surprised. It's as though I see you naked. Have we been summoned here to be insulted? And you, Krishna, why do you agree to this? You're like a dog gnawing a bone he's stolen from a sacrifice. Giving you this place is like giving a woman in heat to a eunuch, or beauty to the blind. Farewell. *Sisupala leaves. Yudhishthira tries to hold him back, in vain.*

YUDHISHTHIRA: Sisupala, king of Tchedi! Everyone here accepts this honor. Take your place with us. *Bhishma then starts speaking. During his narration, Sisupala slowly returns to listen to his own history.*

BHISHMA: I will reveal to you Sisupala's secret; he doesn't know it himself. When he was born, he had four arms and a third eye in the middle of his forehead. He howled like a jackal trapped in a forest fire. His mother and father were thinking of abandoning him when they heard a voice say: "Your son will be prodigiously strong, but one day a king will take him on his knee, his two superfluous arms will drop to the ground, his third eye will disappear, and this king will be the death of your son." The voice ceased. All the kings of the earth came to admire the extraordinary newborn child. His father, trembling, placed him on their laps, one after the other. Nothing happened. One day he was taken to see Krishna, who received him affectionately. He was put on Krishna's knee. At once, two of his arms fell to the ground and his third eye faded away. His mother, terrified, said to Krishna: "I implore you, allow my son a hundred offenses, a hundred offenses deserving death." Krishna in his goodness granted her wish. He is honored by all men of good faith, he is a master and a friend.

SISUPALA: He is not my master and he is not my friend.

BHISHMA: I tell you, everything exists through him. He is the heavens, the sky, the constellations. He is the movement of our lives.

SISUPALA: An old man's beautiful words.

BHISHMA: Sisupala, you are young and you don't want to learn. Can't you see that behind Krishna's smile and his half-closed eyes, death is waiting?

*Bhima suddenly lifts his foot and shouts:*

BHIMA: Come, whoever refuses Krishna the honor my brother has offered, let him draw near. I will put my foot on his head. *Silence. All eyes are on Bhima. Sisupala addresses everyone:*

SISUPALA: What are you all doing looking at a foot? What's so extraordinary about it? It scares you? *To Bhima* Bhima, you think I'm afraid of your foot? *To Bhishma* Bhishma, you are very old and very tired. You always repeat the same weary theme. You have gone mad. How can you reduce the entire universe to one man?

DRONA: Sisupala, this morning you rose from your bed to die.

*Sisupala returns to Bhima:*

SISUPALA: How long are you going to stay like a heron? Stop rolling your big eyes, put your foot on the ground. One puff and you'll fall flat. *Bhima wants to throw himself at Sisupala. His brothers hold him back.*

YUDHISHTHIRA: Bhima!

NAKULA: Not today, not here. *Sisupala, who has drawn his sword, cries:*

SISUPALA: Yes, release him. Let him come!

BHISHMA: Drop your sword!

SISUPALA: *To Bhishma* Don't give me orders! I don't admire you. You talk all the time about justice, but I don't see you honoring an aged wife. You're a storehouse of vows, exhortations, maxims, but as for a son of yours, I keep looking, but I find him nowhere. Your life is barren. You are an impotent old owl living off other birds' eggs, a man who's no more than a woman. Dhritarashtra, the tragedy of your race comes from him. *He indicates Bhishma.* From that idiotic vow of which he is so proud. He has lived long enough. Rise up! Light a fire and burn him, the root of your disease.

BHISHMA: Sisupala, you don't realize it, but your thoughts are sweeping you to your death. You are provoking Krishna. You will end as dust. *Sisupala then turns to Krishna.*

SISUPALA: Yes, I provoke you! Yes, I defy you! I will kill you, and with you all the idiots who adore you and take you for a god. For I adore no one. To your feet! Come and fight! *Krishna, until this moment, had remained smiling, with half-closed eyes. All the kings are still and watch him. He slowly raises his eyelids and says to the assembly:*

KRISHNA: Sisupala is my eternal enemy, my obstinate, faithful enemy. I've had nothing from him—from his kingdom—but attacks, abuse, and broken promises. My tenderness for him has remained unchanged, but he never stops provoking me. He has killed my soldiers, stolen my horses, abducted my wives. I have accepted the hundred offenses I promised his mother. Today he insults me in front of you all and I accept it no longer.

SISUPALA: Accept or not accept, who cares? Your anger can't touch me, nor your tenderness. *As Sisupala is about to throw himself at him, Krishna lifts his hand and a brilliant object appears in it.*

ARJUNA: The disc! *Everything stops. Krishna throws the disc. Sisupala screams, clutches his throat, and falls. Silence. The boy asks Vyasa:*

BOY: He killed him?

VYASA: He has cut off his head without stirring from his place.

BOY: And the other kings?

VYASA: They said nothing, for the earth shook, a thunderbolt shot from the sky, and out of the body of young Sisupala emanated an intense light. The light rose and bowed down before Krishna. Yes, everyone present saw it.

BOY: I can see it.

*Krishna takes up the narrative:*

KRISHNA: Then the light moved toward Krishna and was as though absorbed by him. The kings saw the light become the body of Krishna. Some bit their lips, others wrung their hands, they were all struck dumb. Krishna pointed to the body of Sisupala and said: "Prepare him an honorable burial." Rain fell, then the sky became blue once more. *The kings leave. Arjuna stays by Yudhishthira. Vyasa prepares to withdraw. Yudhishthira keeps him back:*

YUDHISHTHIRA: Vyasa, why this fury in Sisupala? Why did he die so senselessly? What does this mean?

VYASA: Death has entered the heart of kings. We must now expect suffering, madness. You, ponder deeply, don't be afraid of your dreams and watch over the earth.

YUDHISHTHIRA: I should no doubt die myself instead of destroying others. *Arjuna stops Vyasa who is about to leave.*

ARJUNA: Vyasa, do you know the end of your poem?

VYASA: I'm not sure it has an end.

ARJUNA: Are you sure, at least, if death catches up with us all, that someone someday will survive?

VYASA: Yes, I am sure. I even have the proof: this child who accompanies me and questions me, and to whom I relate the chaos of the past.

# THE GAME OF DICE

*Duryodhana bursts onto the stage in fury. As he speaks, his monologue comes to life, the Pandavas appearing and playing their parts in his story.*

DURYODHANA: Everything I saw there drives me mad. . . . I saw their palace, it was divine, sublime—unequalled anywhere—because the architect was a god, Maya himself. A palace no one could rival. Arjuna said to me:

ARJUNA: Look at the crystal walls, the turquoise ceiling, those streaks of sunlight are golden beams.

DURYODHANA: And I saw them. Yes, I saw the sand of pearls, the terraces carved in moonstone, and suddenly I ran into an invisible wall! Arjuna laughed and said:

ARJUNA: That's Maya's masterpiece, you think of a wall and the wall's there.

DURYODHANA: I go farther, suddenly Bhima shouts:

BHIMA: Watch out! There's a pool in front of you!

DURYODHANA: A pool! I don't see any pool. Yet my feet are wet! I run, I open a door, there's no door, I crash into a wall, I hurt myself and Draupadi cries out:

DRAUPADI: He's blind. Blind father, blind son! *At this moment, Gandhari appears and Duryodhana continues his narrative for her to hear.*

DURYODHANA: I roll down a staircase and fall into a cistern. With a splash! And a splash of laughter, cruel laughter! Bhima, wolf-belly, jeered at me. Draupadi laughed; her laugh cut me to the heart. All that . . . *He does not complete his sentence, it is as though he comes out of a dream. Now he is back in his own palace. Someone new (Sakuni) has just entered.*

GANDHARI: Who is it?

SAKUNI: It's Sakuni. Your brother.

GANDHARI: What are you doing here?

SAKUNI: I've come to see my nephews.

GANDHARI: They are bitter and restless. Duryodhana, my eldest son, doesn't eat, doesn't sleep. . . .

SAKUNI: Why?

DURYODHANA: Because I've seen all the kings of the earth surround Yudhishthira. I've seen his people happy, even the aged, even the children. . . . I've seen a head sliced from a body with a flick of Krishna's wrist. Sisupala decapitated; Yudhishthira, king of kings, respected, loved . . . while I, I love nothing, I am nothing. I've nothing left but to throw myself into the fire, or take poison.

SAKUNI: There is a way to ruin Yudhishthira, and I know it.

GANDHARI: What are you hatching?

DURYODHANA: Tell me your way.

SAKUNI: Yudhishthira is a virtuous man—incapable of the tiniest lie—but he has one weakness: he loves gambling. Double weakness, because he loves gambling, but he doesn't know how to play. Challenge him to a game of dice, he won't be able to refuse. But I am here and I know every throw, every dangerous combination. No one can beat me. Let me play in your place, my nephew, and I will win.

DURYODHANA: We must play high.

SAKUNI: We will play high.

DURYODHANA: You think Yudhishthira will accept?

SAKUNI: I'm sure. *Dhritarashtra has just entered. Sakuni addresses him:* Dhritarashtra, I greet you. It's me, Sakuni.

DHRITARASHTRA: Welcome, Sakuni. What do you want?

SAKUNI: To distract your son, let's arrange a game of dice and invite Yudhishthira.

DHRITARASHTRA: They say he plays badly.

SAKUNI: I don't know. I've never seen him play.

DHRITARASHTRA: What do you intend to stake?

DURYODHANA: Whatever he proposes.

DHRITARASHTRA: Gandhari, what do you think of a game of dice?

GANDHARI: Don't touch the game, my son. You have found nothing but love in this palace. You are the eldest, you rule over everyone. What more do you want?

DURYODHANA: A man says: "I've enough to eat and wear, I need nothing more." Shame! He says: "I don't know anger." Shame! No, I am like a dried-up stream; like a wooden elephant, useless and rejected. All because my father was born blind, because one doesn't give a throne to a blind man. I'm not a man, not even a woman. Everything I've seen there drives me mad. The massive gold vases, the arms, the chariots, the precious stones, the long lines of cattle before the gates, the thousands of women. The savage kings come tamely, bearing treasures and bending the knee. The best of all existence is there. The agony of it tore me from life—I lost my senses, I fell to the ground. . . .

GANDHARI: Calm yourself. Send for your wives.

DURYODHANA: But I want to be discontented! Dissatisfied! A man's body grows from birth and everyone is delighted. In the same way, his desire grows, his desire for power. I have doubts about myself. Sometimes I even question my value. I must resolve these doubts.

GANDHARI: You have a shadow in your mind. It sweeps you away with incredible force.

SAKUNI: *To Dhritarashtra* Why refuse a simple game of dice? The gods created the world as a game. Insects play with flowers, the stars dance their secret patterns in the sky. Why, Dhritarashtra, must you always frown on pleasure? *Dhritarashtra turns and calls:*

DHRITARASHTRA: Dushassana is there? Dushassana! *Dushassana approaches:*

DUSHASSANA: I am here.

DHRITARASHTRA: Take a horse. Go invite Yudhishthira—tell him we are playing dice amongst friends.

SAKUNI: Tell him we're playing the Gate of Paradise. It's his favorite game.

DUSHASSANA: I leave at once.

DHRITARASHTRA: When Bhishma and Drona are at my side, I'm safe from harm.

*They leave and it grows dark. Bhishma appears, carrying a lamp. He watches them move away, sits down. All is quiet. Bhishma then speaks, as though to himself.*

BHISHMA: Why do you wish to see me in secret? *At this moment Krishna can be seen. He goes to Bhishma, saying:*

KRISHNA: Bhishma, you have lived more than four-score years. You have seen generations come and go. But you have no wrinkles, your flesh stays firm, your voice is strong, your clear mind reflects the depth of your thought.

BHISHMA: Where are you leading me Krishna?

KRISHNA: A game of dice is being prepared.

BHISHMA: I know.

KRISHNA: Yudhishthira will not turn down the invitation.

BHISHMA: He should not come.

KRISHNA: Whatever his reasons for playing, he will come.

BHISHMA: This game of dice hides storms that I distinguish badly.

KRISHNA: So do I.

BHISHMA: What do you want?

KRISHNA: Bhishma, here your authority is not disputed. If I come like a shadow to speak with you, it is to ask a favor: whatever you see in the course of the game, whatever you hear, you must not interrupt the match.

BHISHMA: In no circumstances?

KRISHNA: In no circumstances.

BHISHMA: If, like me, you have difficulty in determining the consequences of this game, wouldn't it be better to avoid the worst?

KRISHNA: What is the worst? *Bhishma reflects before replying.*

BHISHMA: Destruction.

KRISHNA: Destruction of what?

BHISHMA: Of the way of truth, of the order of the world—destruction of dharma, that's the worst.

KRISHNA: And if your race has to be destroyed, so as to save dharma? *Bhishma stays silent. Krishna insists:* Would you be ready to sacrifice your race? What is your answer?

BHISHMA: That question is with me always—sharpening my thoughts, destroying my sleep, making my heart pound all night long.

KRISHNA: That's why I ask you not to intervene. Let each one go to his limit.

*The lights return. As Krishna disappears into the shadow, the other characters reappear. Yudhishthira, accompanied by his four brothers, enters Dhritarashtra's palace. They exchange greetings and the game is prepared. Sakuni takes his place opposite Yudhishthira. All the court are present.*

SAKUNI: Let us agree on a covenant before the first throw.

YUDHISHTHIRA: Sakuni, it's you who are going to play?

SAKUNI: Yes, I'm playing for my nephew.

YUDHISHTHIRA: You spend your life playing. People have seen you perform unbelievable tricks, but cheating is a crime. You are not going to lead us like a thief into a crooked lane?

SAKUNI: The powerful player who knows how to play and who ponders calmly is not worried by cheating. Here there is no crime, only the game, nothing but the game. A wise man debates with fools. Do you call that cheating? A seasoned warrior fights against beginners; you call that cheating? Science is not cheating. You always enter a game with a wish to win. That's how life is. No cheat can ever defeat a master. Withdraw from the match if you are afraid. *Yudhishthira takes a necklace from his neck.*

YUDHISHTHIRA: Here is a gold necklace, and pearls without equal churned in the vortex of the ocean. *Duryodhana takes a necklace himself and throws it beside the one from Yudhishthira.*

DURYODHANA: Sakuni, win me this game. *Yudhishthira and Sakuni throw the dice.*

SAKUNI: I have won.

DURYODHANA: I have pearls and gold. That's not what I want.

YUDHISHTHIRA: I have immense treasures—gold and jewels locked in four hundred coffers. This wealth is mine. I play it against you. *Duryodhana assents. They throw the dice.*

SAKUNI: I've won.

YUDHISHTHIRA: I have a hundred thousand female slaves; young, beautiful, perfumed, trained in sixty-four skills, expert in song and dance. I play them against you. *Duryodhana indicates his agreement. Sakuni and Yudhishthira throw the dice.*

SAKUNI: I have won.

YUDHISHTHIRA: Swift-fingered Sakuni, I have as many male slaves; obedient, adroit, dressed in the finest silk. I now play them against you. *They throw the dice.*

SAKUNI: I have won. *Gandhari then says to Dhritarashtra:*

GANDHARI: The dice have turned their heads. Stop them! Bhishma, stop this game. One word from you will suffice.

DURYODHANA: I know your mind, Bhishma. You are with our enemies.

BHISHMA: You think you are winning, but you are the loser.

GANDHARI: Command them to stop! *Everyone awaits Bhishma's reaction. He remains silent.* You say nothing? Why? Give the order! *Duryodhana then asks Yudhishthira:*

DURYODHANA: Yudhishthira, do you want us to stop the game?

YUDHISHTHIRA: No. Let's proceed.

SAKUNI: What's your stake?

YUDHISHTHIRA: I have sixteen thousand chariots with golden shafts, harnessed to splendid steeds. I add two Gandharva stallions mottled like partridges, given to me by a demigod. This wealth is mine. I play them against you. *Yudhishthira throws the dice. Sakuni plays his turn.*

SAKUNI: I've won again. What have you left?

YUDHISHTHIRA: My studfarms, my stables, my cows, my bulls, my goats, my ewes. *They throw the dice.*

SAKUNI: I have won.

YUDHISHTHIRA: My capital, my lands, my forests, my kingdom, my people, all that I possess. *They throw the dice.*

SAKUNI: I have won. I have won everything. *They all start to leave. Yudhishthira is silent, motionless.*

DURYODHANA: You still have something left?

YUDHISHTHIRA: I still have my brothers Nakula and Sahadeva, the twins with golden eyes, the sons of Madri. They are beyond all value. I play them against you. *Duryodhana signals to his brother Dushassana who comes beside him as his stake. Sakuni and Yudhishthira throw the dice.*

SAKUNI: I have won. Madri's sons are ours.

YUDHISHTHIRA: I still have Arjuna, he who can never lose, Krishna's friend, his brother by marriage. For him the snakes opened up their secret world. He was loved by a Naga queen in a great palace under the sea. When he plucks the cord of his bow, Gandiva, every living creature trembles. No man, no woman can resist him. He's as precious to me as life. I now play him against you. *Dushassana remains as Duryodhana's stake. The two players throw the dice. Arjuna makes a sharp accusing sign as though he has seen Sakuni cheat. Sakuni plays again.*

SAKUNI: I've won.

YUDHISHTHIRA: I still have Bhima, built like a lion, the mightiest of men. He tears out trees by the roots, he makes the earth shake, he has carried his four brothers and his mother on his shoulders, he is strength itself. I play him against you. *Yudhishthira plays. Sakuni puts the dice into Bhima's hand and indicates that he should play for himself. He throws the dice.*

SAKUNI: I've won. Have you still something left?

YUDHISHTHIRA: Of all my brothers, I remain alone. I play myself, Yudhishthira. I stake myself. *Sakuni looks at Duryodhana, who places himself next to Sakuni. Sakuni is ready to play when Yudhishthira takes the dice and puts them in Duryodhana's hand, to force him to play for himself. After a moment of panic, Duryodhana returns the dice to Sakuni, who plays.*

SAKUNI: I have won, and nothing is worse than to lose oneself for, when one loses everything, freedom is the only wealth that remains. But you have one last possession and you forget it.

YUDHISHTHIRA: What?

SAKUNI: You possess a wife. She is the only treasure I have not won. Stake Draupadi and win back everything, thanks to her.

YUDHISHTHIRA: She's a woman who is neither too short nor too tall, neither pale nor dark. Her hair falls in blue-black waves; no lotus shines like her eyes. She is the earth's most perfect creation and the pole of all men's desire. The last to sleep, the first to wake, before the shepherds. Under the glistening sweat, her skin is smooth. I play her against you. *Sakuni and Yudhishthira throw the dice.*

DHRITARASHTRA: Who has lost? Who has lost?

SAKUNI: Once again, Yudhishthira has lost.

DURYODHANA: Dushassana, quick, bring Draupadi here. Hurry. We'll put her in the scullery to scrape the dishes. *Dushassana goes to find Draupadi who is waiting in another room of the palace.*

DUSHASSANA: Draupadi . . .

DRAUPADI: Yes, what do you want?

DUSHASSANA: The game of dice is over.

DRAUPADI: And?

DUSHASSANA: You are requested to come to the palace.

DRAUPADI: Who requests me? Why?

DUSHASSANA: Because Yudhishthira has lost you.

DRAUPADI: What do you mean, he has lost me?

DUSHASSANA: He has lost you at dice.

DRAUPADI: Had he nothing else to play?

DUSHASSANA: He played all he had and lost it all—his wealth, his cattle, his kingdom, his brothers. He even played and lost himself.

DRAUPADI: He lost himself?

DUSHASSANA: That's what I said.

DRAUPADI: Before losing me, or after?

DUSHASSANA: Before losing you.

DRAUPADI: Return to the hall and ask him this: is it true that you lost yourself first, before losing me? And if you yourself were already lost, had you the right to play me? *Dushassana tries to grab hold of Draupadi:*

DUSHASSANA: You were staked and lost. You are ours. Come!

DRAUPADI: Allow me to dress! I have only one robe and it is stained with blood. I'm in my period. Don't show me in this state to the kings.

DUSHASSANA: That it's your period, that you only have one dress, who cares? We have won you at dice, you are now no more than a slave. Enough, come! *He takes her by the hair and drags her to the hall.*

DRAUPADI: What does this mean? What have I done? I despise you, I hate you. Madman, let me go! Don't drag me in front of all those men! *They arrive in the hall and Dushassana throws her on the floor. Duryodhana and Karna laugh noisily. The Pandavas do not move. Bhishma and Drona are expressionless.*

DUSHASSANA: Here is the new servant! *Draupadi lifts her face and looks around her.*

DRAUPADI: There isn't even a breath of life in Bhishma, in Drona? They see this shame and do nothing. Yudhishthira, had you the right to lose me? If you were lost before playing me, I was no longer yours. Can one belong to someone who has lost himself? Who can answer me? Bhishma, answer me!

BHISHMA: I am troubled. The question is obscure.

BHIMA: Yudhishthira, one plays for women in a brothel, but one still has pity for them. Bring me fire and I'll burn your hands!

NAKULA: Bhima, be calm and listen.

DRONA: When Yudhishthira made this wager, he had already lost his self, so he could not play his wife.

DURYODHANA: Error! She was designated by name, and well and truly won.

KARNA: Draupadi satisfies five men, she is clearly public property. Everyone agrees, she has been fairly won.

BHISHMA: If a man loses what isn't his, he loses in a dream. . . .

DHRITARASHTRA: Gandhari, what do you say?

GANDHARI: Draupadi, like all women, made no distinction between her husband and herself. She was part of him, she was him. Whether he lost her before or after, I don't see the difference. Draupadi has been won. I regret to have to say it, but it is so.

DURYODHANA: Everything has been won—their clothes down to the last clasp. Come, strip them naked! All of them! *They start to remove their clothes.*

KARNA: And Draupadi as well, we want to see her naked.

DURYODHANA: Dushassana, take off her robe. *Dushassana starts to pull at her robe. She implores Krishna:*

DRAUPADI: Krishna, Govinda, wherever you are, you see a woman treated with contempt. Janardana, Mahayogi, help me, my reason's failing. Krishna, raise your hand to save me. I know you can. *Krishna appears and holds out his hand toward her.*

BHIMA: Listen to what I say. May the way to heaven be closed to me forever if I break my word. When the battle comes, I will smash Dushassana's chest and I'll drink his blood. I swear I will. I will eat his guts and drink his blood.

DURYODHANA: Don't bellow! You only frighten the flies. *Dushassana pulls savagely on the robe, but the robe, as it unfolds, seems interminable, infinitely long. A heap of material is growing in the middle of the room. Bhishma cries:*

BHISHMA: Silence. Watch. A miracle is taking place under our eyes.

DHRITARASHTRA: What? What is it?

GANDHARI: Bhishma, what is this miracle?

BHISHMA: Her dress is endless, impossible to strip her naked. It's a prodigy of Krishna.

DURYODHANA: A prodigy? Where do you see a prodigy? She's wearing layers and layers of cloth. Stop, Dushassana, let her go! *Dushassana falls to the ground, exhausted, while Duryodhana adds:* Take her away! I've already told you, put her with the slaves to scrape dishes. *Duryodhana takes Draupadi by the arm. She resists.*

DRAUPADI: Wait! Let me go! You can't do that to me! The wind has never seen me. The sun has never seen me in my own palace. And here I am, exposed before you all. Where is dharma? Where is the truth? What has been violated? Nothing is clear. Tell me whether I am, or whether I am not, a slave, a gambler's prize. If I am a slave, say so and I submit, but say so clearly.

BHISHMA: There's only one person who can answer you: Yudhishthira himself.

DURYODHANA: Good idea. Ask him. Let him say if he was or if he wasn't your master. If he wasn't your master, I let you free. *To Yudhishthira* You don't answer? *Yudhishthira stays silent.*

KARNA: Draupadi, go down to the kitchens. Your new masters are here. Choose a new husband. *To Bhima, who wants to intervene:* And you, hold your tongue. You don't own yourself anymore. You haven't even the right to be angry.

DURYODHANA: Draupadi, you want another man. Look at my thigh!

DHRITARASHTRA: Bhishma, speak to me! What should I do?

BHISHMA: A doomed man gradually loses his reason without noticing it; he no longer sees things as they are. Death has already cut into his life.

DURYODHANA: These words are aimed at me?

BHISHMA: Yes, at you as well.

DRAUPADI: Duryodhana, Dushassana, and all your brothers—and you also Karna, you also Sakuni—you are lost. A savage death will drag you to the ground and your blood will drench the earth. Dushassana, my hair will stay unbound until your death. I will wash my hair in your blood. And you, Duryodhana, death will strike you in the thigh. *Somewhere, an animal cries. They all shiver.*

GANDHARI: A jackal cried.

BHISHMA: Yes, near the temple.

DHRITARASHTRA: Draupadi, come close. Choose a favor; whatever you wish and I grant it. What do you choose?

DRAUPADI: That Yudhishthira be free.

DHRITARASHTRA: He is free. But you deserve a second favor. Choose.

DRAUPADI: That Bhima, Arjuna, Nakula, and Sahadeva be free.

DHRITARASHTRA: They are free. But you deserve a third favor. Choose.

DRAUPADI: No. I don't wish for a third favor.

DHRITARASHTRA: Why?

DRAUPADI: Because greed devours all beings and is dharma's ruin. I refuse greed. Save my husbands.

GANDHARI: You ask nothing for yourself?

DRAUPADI: No. I want nothing, above all no favor.

KARNA: Her husbands were drowning. Draupadi is the raft that saves them.

YUDHISHTHIRA: *To Dhritarashtra* Now, what should we do?

DHRITARASHTRA: Look at me. I agreed to this match so as to meet my friends and also to measure the weakness of my children. You didn't answer insult with insult, that is good. Have no fear, Yudhishthira. Go toward happiness; take back your clothes and leave in freedom.

*The Pandavas and Draupadi pick up their clothes and leave.*

DURYODHANA: Don't let them go—otherwise it's war. We cheated, they know it, they can never forgive us. Arjuna tightens his bow, Bhima raises his club. They want to recover everything; they are already preparing a massacre. Call them back, let's play a final round. If they lose, let them spend twelve years in the forest, we will have time to fortify. Father, call them back, they are marching toward our death.

DHRITARASHTRA: Yes, call them back. My son is right. Better a game than a war. *Dushassana goes to call back the Pandavas. Gandhari addresses the blind king, her husband:*

GANDHARI: Reject that son who wishes to ruin you. Re-establish your authority. Don't vacillate. You will destroy your family.

DHRITARASHTRA: Very well. My family will be destroyed. I cannot prevent it any longer. *Dushassana catches up with the Pandavas who are leaving the palace.*

DUSHASSANA: One moment.

YUDHISHTHIRA: What do you want?

DUSHASSANA: You are recalled for a final match. The hall is ready. *Yudhishthira stops, seems to think. His brothers and Draupadi press him to continue.*

DRAUPADI: You hesitate?

YUDHISHTHIRA: What does this call of destiny conceal?

ARJUNA: Leave destiny alone. We need to make ourselves strong, to recover our possessions, all that we have lost.

NAKULA: Come. Give me your hand.

YUDHISHTHIRA: *To Dushassana* You say the hall is ready?

DUSHASSANA: Yes, for the final round. The carpet, the table, the dice, all is ready. With one throw you can win back your wealth, your kingdom, and more besides. With one throw. *Yudhishthira seems uncertain.*

BHIMA: Leave this place. Trust me.

ARJUNA: Yudhishthira, you're in a dream. It leads to darkness.

DRAUPADI: Come with us.

YUDHISHTHIRA: No. I must play.

DRAUPADI: Why?

YUDHISHTHIRA: I can't refuse my rivals a last chance of salvation.

ARJUNA: What are you saying?

YUDHISHTHIRA: If they take everything from us, they will be the losers. Draupadi, you said so yourself. Sakuni condemns to death those who asked him to cheat. I repeat, I cannot deny them a chance of salvation. *To Dushassana* I follow you. *Instantly, Yudhishthira, his brothers, and Draupadi are back in the hall.*

SAKUNI: We will play one single throw. Listen carefully: if we lose, we will spend twelve years in the forest clothed in rags, and a thirteenth year in an unknown place, hidden and disguised. If, during the course of the thirteenth year, we are discovered, we will spend a further twelve years in the woods. If you lose, the exile is yours. At the end of thirteen years, the one or the other will regain his kingdom.

YUDHISHTHIRA: Let's play.

SAKUNI: All our treasures, all our women, all our lands, all our herds against exile in the forest.

YUDHISHTHIRA: Let's play. *They throw the dice. Sakuni's gesture shows that he has won.*

DUSHASSANA: They have lost, the Pandavas! They thought they were on top of the world and now they are cast out into the forest, into the desert. They will gnaw roots and chew weeds, with shriveled skin and filthy beards. Draupadi, choose a husband amongst us. Yours are now trees without sap, animals stuffed with straw.

BHIMA: One day I will remind you of your words and I'll drink your blood, vile·swine. *Dushassana goes around him, imitating his heavy gait and mocking him.*

DUSHASSANA: The big beast! The great ox! Oo! Oo! *Duryodhana and Karna laugh with Dushassana.*

BHIMA: Dushassana, I will open your belly, and Arjuna will kill Karna. *Arjuna advances toward Karna.*

ARJUNA: Yes, I'll kill Karna. I said so and I will do it.

KARNA: I will always be ahead of you. Don't forget to take your bow into the woods and practice.

ARJUNA: I won't forget.

KARNA: And each day I will think of your death.

ARJUNA: Death, Karna . . . each of your thoughts, each breath brings you nearer to death. I made a vow, I'll say no more. *Karna, Duryodhana, and Dushassana withdraw, accompanied by Sakuni. Kunti then appears going to Yudhishthira and asking:*

KUNTI: My son, answer me, for everyone is asking the same question: why did you agree to play? *Yudhishthira does not reply.* What drew you? Pleasure? Vice? Fear? To avoid war at all costs?

YUDHISHTHIRA: Now we must go.

KUNTI: But what was the cause of this calamity? Who could have imagined it? Such a disaster, in so short a time. *To Arjuna* And you?

Why this obsession with Karna? Why do you need to kill him? What happened? I don't understand. *Arjuna does not reply.*

BHISHMA: Kunti, you can't follow them into exile. You will live with me. *As the Pandavas leave, Kunti is still saying to them:*

KUNTI: Starving, naked, what will you live off in the woods?

*The Pandavas have left with Draupadi. Kunti also leaves, on Bhishma's arm. Only Dhritarashtra, Gandhari, Vyasa, and the boy remain. Ganesha reappears.*

DHRITARASHTRA: Vyasa!

VYASA: I am here.

DHRITARASHTRA: Describe their departure.

VYASA: They walk barefooted. The whole city watches them in silence. Yudhishthira walks ahead. Then comes Bhima, with staring eyes fixed on his two arms. With each step he takes, Arjuna stirs up clouds of sand. Sahadeva and Nakula are soiled with dust and mud from head to foot. Draupadi is last, her head bowed toward the ground.

DHRITARASHTRA: Why? What do these attitudes mean?

VYASA: Bhima is contracting his arms, the most powerful arms in the world. In the grains of sand he scatters, Arjuna sees a thousand arrows fly. The twins hide their beauty so that no woman should be tempted to follow.

GANDHARI: And Draupadi murmurs, in her blood-stained robe, "One day we will see widows, their children dead, their hair unbound, on the day of their period, honoring cold corpses with their cries."

VYASA: I can't see them anymore. *The king and queen leave. Ganesha, alone with Vyasa and the boy, picks up the dice. They play together.*

# PART II

# EXILE IN
# THE FOREST

# THE PANDAVAS IN DANGER

*Duryodhana is seated on his bed in his palace. His brother, Dushassana, asleep in the same room, wakes abruptly and runs over to him. It is dawn.*

DUSHASSANA: Duryodhana!

DURYODHANA: Yes, what?

DUSHASSANA: My dreams are poisoning me. I've seen Yudhishthira and his brothers, out of all proportion, huge, clutching winged demons and swarming toward us. Arjuna became a tower, sneering and belching smoke. Bhima had red teeth, I saw blood-stained words streaming from his mouth and he cried "You dragged my wife by the hair. I will tear open your belly, I will eat your guts."

DURYODHANA: Calm down. Give me your hands.

DUSHASSANA: Our enemies are growing stronger. We must attack them, now. We must destroy them; otherwise very soon it will be too late.

DURYODHANA: Dushassana, my brother, their exile protects them. The game they lost protects them. I am bound by its rule.

DUSHASSANA: Yes, but the Pandavas are stamping the rules into dust. I know it; they are preparing for war. Night and the forests are on their side. You must preserve your empire. You must kill them. Announce a hunt. You can say they died in an accident. I will help you. *Dhritarashtra and Gandhari appear at this moment. Seeing them, the two brothers stop speaking.*

DHRITARASHTRA: I hear breathing. Who's there?

DURYODHANA: Your sons. I'm with Dushassana.

GANDHARI: Up so early? *Duryodhana embraces his mother and announces:*

DURYODHANA: We're preparing a hunt.

DHRITARASHTRA: What game?

DURYODHANA: Stag. Fowl.

DUSHASSANA: Boar.

DHRITARASHTRA: I know your voices. What's disturbing you?

DUSHASSANA: A bad night.

DHRITARASHTRA: Yes . . .

GANDHARI: We wander through the palace from room to room. But even sleep's been banished.

DHRITARASHTRA: All the time I think of them, out there, miserable, wretched, ravaged by fever, pining for the past. . . .

DURYODHANA: I think of nothing else. I spend all my nights with them. I see them in the dark, close to me, like shadows—but strong, stronger and stronger. Exile strengthens them, I know it. Friends and allies are rallying. They are stocking arms, all they speak of is my death.

DHRITARASHTRA: My son, your reign is a good reign. Don't let your anguish destroy it.

DURYODHANA: If my reign is a good reign, where is your sleep? Power is brief. Yes, I'm disturbed, anguished. . . . *Duryodhana and Dushassana leave. Alone with Dhritarashtra, Gandhari says to him:*

GANDHARI: He's right. You have given him your power because you can't rule the world in the dark. Well, if your son is your king, let him rule. Trust him and stop pacing through the palace all night long.

DHRITARASHTRA: In his heart, he's blind and he attracts disaster.

GANDHARI: If danger is approaching the Pandavas in the forest, warn them, send them a secret message. *Dhritarashtra hesitates an instant, then goes out saying:*

DHRITARASHTRA: No, I can't betray my son. No. Not that.

# IN THE FOREST

*The five Pandavas and Draupadi, barefooted and ill-clothed, appear in the forest. Draupadi constructs a little altar with flowers and sticks. Bhima breaks wood.*

*A young woman (Amba) enters. Her clothes are in tatters, her hair wild and dusty. As she appears, a heavy stake in her hand, she cries:*

AMBA: Where is Bhima? I'm looking for Bhima! Where is Bhima? Bhima!

BHIMA: I am Bhima. What do you want?

AMBA: I was told I would find you in the forest and that you are the strongest man in the world.

BHIMA: It's true.

AMBA: You must fight for me.

BHIMA: Against whom?

AMBA: Against an old man, a proud and ferocious old man, against Bhishma!

BHIMA: Bhishma? Impossible! I love and respect him. No one would risk himself against him.

ARJUNA: He can only die if he wishes for death. He is invincible. *Yudhishthira asks the young girl:*

YUDHISHTHIRA: Who are you?

AMBA: I am Amba. Because of Bhishma, long ago the world rejected me.

DRAUPADI: You are really Amba?

YUDHISHTHIRA: It was more than forty years ago. . . .

AMBA: Hate keeps me young. I live only to kill Bhishma. I swore it. But all the men to whom I turn, even you Bhima, even you Arjuna, you all tell me he can't be killed. Nonetheless, I will kill him. To find the moment that ends his life, I have all eternity.

YUDHISHTHIRA: Rest. Free yourself from this wish to kill.

DRAUPADI: *To Yudhishthira* Why do you always propose peace, forgiveness?
*To Amba*
Amba, don't search only in this world. Pray to the demigods, call on invisible forces.

AMBA: For forty years I have been searching everywhere. No force can outwit death. *Somewhere in the forest, a voice calls:*

VOICE: Except death itself.

AMBA: Who spoke? Who said "except death itself"? Who is hiding behind the trees? *No one answers. Amba asks again:*

AMBA: How can death outwit death? Explain, don't leave me in this void. *The voice stays silent. Then Draupadi asks Amba, who prepares to resume her wandering:*

DRAUPADI: Would you like to eat?

AMBA: I only eat what the wind brings. I never sleep. All my life I walk and question. I need nothing. *She goes. Draupadi says:*

DRAUPADI: Someone is laughing at us.

YUDHISHTHIRA: What are you saying?

DRAUPADI: A magician has made us blind, he's torturing us.

YUDHISHTHIRA: What magician?

DRAUPADI: We had a kingdom. Or did I dream it? *No one answers her. Addressing Yudhishthira, she resumes:*

DRAUPADI: Yudhishthira, I saw you on a throne, you were perfumed and radiant, and now I see an anxious man squatting on a heap of weeds. And with you, your brothers, my husbands. Look at them. *The other brothers have ceased all activity. They listen motionless, heads bowed.*

DRAUPADI: I was dragged in front of everyone clothed in a single robe, stained with my blood. The sight of a woman made men laugh. My husbands were there. I had given each of them a son. I needed their aid and Duryodhana is still alive! I despise your strength. *No one answers her. She adds:* I have another question. . . . *Yudhishthira raises his eyes and watches her.*

DRAUPADI: You are just, you have no pride, you only speak words of truth. How did the idea of the game take hold of you? How could you agree to play? And lose everything? Even your brothers? Even your wife? I don't understand. *Yudhishthira does not reply. He is absorbed in drawing a pattern on the ground. Draupadi comes over to him.*

DRAUPADI: Sometimes I tell myself a man is nothing, he has his nature imposed upon him, nothing comes from himself. He is like a tree that falls into a river and is swept away; like a bull led by a string of pearls threaded through the nose. All that we think, all that we say is just a game, just moving shadows. Yes, I suspect a magician. Destiny is vicious. It plays tricks on us and the creator himself takes sides. I condemn him.

YUDHISHTHIRA: I have the same questions as you, Draupadi. Why is this act rewarded and this one not? No one can answer, it's the secret of all time.

DRAUPADI: And you bow down before this monster?

YUDHISHTHIRA: Whether there is a reward or not, with all my strength I do what I must do. That is my dharma. It's my only raft. Without this obligation, nothing would be stable anymore and the world would lose its honor—in darkness.

DRAUPADI: Your dharma forced you to play? *Yudhishthira does not answer.* I have more than love for you, I have respect, since the very first day. But something in your heart eludes me and saps my strength. A man who doesn't know why he is alive, where is his will? What hope sustains him? Happiness is for the man who acts.

YUDHISHTHIRA: And if silence was necessary for the harmony of the world. Silence, solitude, thought . . . *Nakula takes up the argument:*

NAKULA: The peasant tends the earth with his plough, next he sows, then he waits, arms folded. The crop will come from the clouds. If the rains don't fall, he won't blame himself, he will say, "I worked like the others, the rain did not come, it's not my fault." But if he hadn't worked, if he hadn't sown, what fruit could he expect?

DRAUPADI: Rise up! Take your weapons! Don't leave us in this desert! *Bhima, who has been listening attentively, now intervenes and says to his brother:*

BHIMA: Yudhishthira, we all want what is good, that's natural. Money, for example, wealth, all the abundance of the earth, that's good, that's excellent; and love, that's delicious, sometimes that's divine. One says it softens the brain, but I say: my brother, there's nothing like love, it's honey, it's bliss, it's the rarest of fruits, love well-made can lead to wisdom. You, you know dharma better than anyone. Your thought follows dharma like a shadow. But wealth? Will you hold out a begging bowl and enjoy wealth? And love? Will you sit alone in a bush and enjoy love? Get up! You must protect the earth. That's the truth and to defend the earth by fasting and moaning is like hoping to gallop by scratching the ear of a mule.

YUDHISHTHIRA: The truth, Bhima, is that I played dice to take away Duryodhana's kingdom.

NAKULA: I don't believe you. Yudhishthira, you can't answer lies with silence. Our kingdom and our power are in the hands of a thief!

BHIMA: You've made a pact with death.

YUDHISHTHIRA: Me?

BHIMA: Yes. It's clear, you take death around with you everywhere. He is one of the family, in front of your eyes.

YUDHISHTHIRA: What are you talking about?

BHIMA: Your energy is dissipated. Death is sitting beside you. You are like an invisible man, a useless burden on the earth. If you have such a taste for misery, why impose it on your wife, your brothers? As for me, I just run around aimlessly for the sake of running. At night, no sleep. Look at Arjuna, his head bowed, his arms flabby. Nakula and Sahadeva turned to stone, and you withered, wild-eyed, like a poor idiot crawling round his chair. I've an idea: it is said that for a man in meditation a year goes by like a day. We've been rotting here for thirteen months. Let's say these thirteen months have gone by like thirteen years! Arise! *Yudhishthira gets to his feet.*

YUDHISHTHIRA: The sons of Dhritarashtra cannot be beaten. Their coffers are full and they have many kings on their side. We are five beggars with hardly the rags we wear. *Draupadi and Bhima remain silent. Yudhishthira goes toward Draupadi.*

YUDHISHTHIRA: One day, Draupadi, wolves and birds will laugh while eating our enemies' flesh, the flesh of those who laughed when they saw you played for and lost. Vultures and jackals will drag away their limbs, the limbs of those who dragged you by the hair. One day, in twelve years, when the time is ripe, but not before. *All remain silent, touched by the firmness of his words. At this moment, Arjuna, who has said nothing, rises. All turn toward him. He goes to embrace Bhima who asks:*

BHIMA: Why do you embrace me?

ARJUNA: Because I am going. *He embraces Nakula and Sahadeva, adding:* I cannot wait here any longer. My arms are weak and my will is slackening. A sickness creeps toward my heart.

YUDHISHTHIRA: Where are you going? *Arjuna embraces Yudhishthira and answers:*

ARJUNA: Somewhere in the north there are weapons. I am going to find them as those we have will not be sufficient.

DRAUPADI: You leave me here?

ARJUNA: Yes, with my brothers. I must go alone.

NAKULA: Where are these weapons?

ARJUNA: Humans do not know them. They are buried deep in the mountains. They say that to obtain them you must forget everything, even your body, even your life. I am ready. *He collects himself for a moment, then adds:* I am going, because ever since childhood I have been marked for war. All the gifts I have received, all the secrets I have learned, have only one aim, one end: war. And now I know that one day this war will come and I will lead it. I know it. I won't miss out on my life. *Nakula gives him his bow.*

DRAUPADI: How long without seeing you?

ARJUNA: I don't know. I've said all I know. I will be back. *He embraces Draupadi and goes. When he has gone, Yudhishthira takes Draupadi in his arms.*

YUDHISHTHIRA: I know you love him in particular. When the time came to be alone with him, your eyes had a special glow, we all noticed it. But he couldn't stay inactive any longer, and however far he goes, we will see him again, even stronger than before.

*The Pandavas and Draupadi lie down while Bhima announces:*

BHIMA: I will watch over your rest. Sleep in peace. *They are all asleep except Bhima, on guard by the fire. Strange cackles and grunts come from the forest and two vague yet frightening shapes emerge from the depths of the night. They are two Rakshasas, hideous demons, a male and a female. The male Rakshasa sniffs the wind and says in a deep, hoarse voice:*

RAKSHASA: Hidimbi, my sister, I think I'm dreaming. . . .

HIDIMBI: What about?

RAKSHASA: Don't you taste tiny droplets of flesh in the wind?

HIDIMBI: Yes, brother, I smell them, I smell human flesh. . . .

RAKSHASA: Look! *They catch sight of the sleepers.*

HIDIMBI: Mmm. . . . My tongue slips smoothly across my lips.

RAKSHASA: Mine, too. I'm split with hunger. Mmm . . . I can already feel the globs of grease in my mouth. . . .

HIDIMBI: Mmm . . . I'm going to plunge my teeth into this flesh, drink their young, hot, steaming, delicious blood. . . .

RAKSHASA: Go and see who they are and bring me their corpses. Hurry! When we have eaten, we'll dance in the moonlight. *Hidimbi goes toward the sleepers but suddenly stops before Bhima. He senses a presence in the shadows and is on his guard. Hidimbi asks him in a quiet voice:*

HIDIMBI: Who are you, you I see?

BHIMA: Bhima. And who are you, you I don't see?

HIDIMBI: My name is Hidimbi, this forest is my kingdom.

BHIMA: You are a Rakshasa?

HIDIMBI: Yes.

BHIMA: Show yourself.

HIDIMBI: No, I don't want to.

BHIMA: Why?

HIDIMBI: I'm not what humans like. I'm black and hairy, and I stink.

BHIMA: I want to see you.

HIDIMBI: No, wait! First I must give myself the face and the body of a gorgeous woman.

BHIMA: You can do that?

HIDIMBI: Look! *She draws herself up and appears as a woman in front of Bhima.*

HIDIMBI: You find me beautiful?

BHIMA: Like the night.

HIDIMBI: Then tell me where you come from, splendid young man. Tell me how you live, what you do.

BHIMA: I watch.

HIDIMBI: This forest is ruled by a terrifying Rakshasa, my brother, who sent me to take your life, but at the sight of you love grasped my soul. You've bewitched me, I love you, I can't kill you. Love me as I love you and be my husband. I fly in the air, I do what I please, I will save you.

BHIMA: I can't be your husband. I already have a wife.

HIDIMBI: Who is she? *Bhima indicates Draupadi asleep in Yudhishthira's arms.*

BHIMA: There.

HIDIMBI: But she's sleeping beside another man. Who is he?

BHIMA: He's my brother. He's also her husband.

HIDIMBI: She has two husbands?

BHIMA: She has five.

HIDIMBI: Five? And you refuse to make me your second wife? What's this riddle? I don't understand.

BHIMA: In any event, I can't follow you. I can't leave them to die.

HIDIMBI: I will save them all.

BHIMA: I don't count on you to save them. No Rakshasa can ever beat me. *The cry of a Rakshasa is heard coming closer.*

HIDIMBI: I hear him. He's running toward us. Quick! Jump on my back, all of you. I'll carry you far from here. You don't know him. He's wild.

BHIMA: I've absolutely no fear of your brother, Hidimbi. Don't look down on me because I'm just a man. . . . *The screaming Rakshasa comes into view. He is huge and terrifying. Those who were asleep, waken. The Rakshasa sees his transformed sister and is furious.*

RAKSHASA: Hidimbi, it's disgusting. You look like a woman. Ah, I understand everything, you vile, depraved pervert. I'm going to kill you and all these slugs as well.

BHIMA: Stop! Before killing this woman, fight with me. With me alone. *The Rakshasa gets ready to attack Bhima. His yells are horrible.*

BHIMA: Yes, yell! I'm going to sew up your horrible jaw. And in a moment, you won't yell anymore.

RAKSHASA: And I will cut you into tiny bits! I will open your belly! I will suck your marrow! I will crunch every crumb in your bones! *The Rakshasa hurls himself onto Bhima, yelling. They fight. Sometimes the Rakshasa has the upper hand, sometimes Bhima.*
    *Hidimbi calls to Bhima:*

HIDIMBI: Dawn is near. It's just before day that the Rakshasa are strongest. Lift him off the ground. Squeeze the wind out of him. Now! *Bhima manages to lift the Rakshasa from the ground.*

BHIMA: I'm going to restore this wood to happiness! *For a moment, Bhima holds the Rakshasa, then throws him to the ground. The demon stops moving little by little. The other Pandavas and Draupadi draw near.*

DRAUPADI: He's dead?

BHIMA: Yes, his monster heart is still. *Hidimbi addresses Yudhishthira:*

HIDIMBI: You are the eldest?

YUDHISHTHIRA: Yes.

HIDIMBI: Listen to me. I know that love is woman's affliction and the time has come for me to suffer. I have chosen your brother, Bhima. If he rejects me, I die. Call me a poor idiot, but grant me this man. *To Draupadi* You have other husbands, give me this one. I want him. If you give him to me, I'll do everything for you, I'll protect you all my life. *Yudhishthira exchanges a look with Draupadi, then replies to Hidimbi:*

YUDHISHTHIRA: Yes! Enjoy my brother Bhima from sunrise to sunset. As long as there's light in the sky, he's yours. But don't forget to bring him back with the dark. *Hidimbi gets up and turns to Bhima:*

HIDIMBI: Are you still afraid of me?

BHIMA: I've never been afraid.

HIDIMBI: What can you still refuse me?

BHIMA: Nothing. *He holds his arms open to Hidimbi.* The sun is rising. Carry me away. I'll stay with you until we're given a son. *They remain immobile in each other's arms while the night's shadows fade and Hidimbi says:*

HIDIMBI: So, transfigured by joy, Hidimbi became a woman of almost incredible beauty. She caught hold of Bhima, she swept him up into the air, and everywhere—on mountain peaks, on sky-blue beaches, in the secret lairs of gazelles, on the shores of forgotten lakes, everywhere—she gave him her love.

BHIMA: They had a son?

HIDIMBI: An enormous son, called Ghatotkatcha. Here he is. *Ghatotkatcha, huge and frightening, has just come out of the night. He takes awkward, tripping steps. Bhima asks Hidimbi:*

BHIMA: It's him? He's our son?

HIDIMBI: Yes, isn't he beautiful?

BHIMA: Already so big? So black?

HIDIMBI: He's a magnificent boy. He has red eyes.

BHIMA: He doesn't seem to know how to walk.

HIDIMBI: He's only just been born. But he'll be very strong, a great magician. I can already feel his power. *Bhima holds out his arms to his son.*

BHIMA: Son, come into my arms! *Ghatotkatcha speaks for the first time, hesitantly:*

GHATOTKATCHA: Father . . .

BHIMA: Yes, it's me. Come . . .

GHATOTKATCHA: Father . . .

BHIMA: Yes, my son. *Abruptly, Ghatotkatcha starts to leave.* Ghatotkatcha, my son, stay with us! *Ghatotkatcha stops for a moment.*

GHATOTKATCHA: I can't.

BHIMA: Why?

GHATOTKATCHA: I live in another world and I must go back with my mother. But if one day you need me, I'll hear your call, I'll be there by your side.

BHIMA: Hidimbi, why not . . . *Hidimbi has returned to her original form, horrifying and repulsive. She interrupts Bhima, hiding her face:*

HIDIMBI: No. Don't look at me. I'm leaving.

BHIMA: Hidimbi! *Hidimbi and Ghatotkatcha leave. Bhima follows them out.*

*Duryodhana appears with his brother, Dushassana, accompanied by others, all very menacing men. They encounter Yudhishthira, then the other brothers and Draupadi.*

YUDHISHTHIRA: Duryodhana . . . What brings you here?

DURYODHANA: I was told that I'd find the king of kings, the supreme ruler in the forest. Could it be you? Caked in mud, with matted hair and leprous hands? *To Dushassana* Dushassana, your dream lied to you. They're impotent, everyone's abandoned them.

DUSHASSANA: No! Don't be deceived! They hide their strength. I feel it in my bones, it's in the air. And Arjuna? Where is Arjuna?

YUDHISHTHIRA: He is on a journey.

DURYODHANA: Wasn't he bound to spend twelve years in the woods? Why has he broken his word? Where is he traveling? With whom?

YUDHISHTHIRA: He is traveling alone. No word has been broken. *Dushassana leaps up, seizes Yudhishthira, puts a dagger to his throat and shouts to Bhima:*

DUSHASSANA: If you come closer, I'll cut your brother's throat. Where is he going? Is he looking for allies? Answer me! *Vyasa appears at this moment, accompanied by the boy. He speaks authoritatively to Dushassana:*

VYASA: Put down that weapon, Dushassana. Obey! *Dushassana looks to Duryodhana who indicates that he should obey. He releases Yudhishthira.*

VYASA: No crime should corrupt this poem. *Yudhishthira straightens, relieved:*

YUDHISHTHIRA: Vyasa, it's a joy to see you again. Thank you. Are you well?

DRAUPADI: What do people say about us? Are we missed?

VYASA: Some miss you, others forget you. I am quite well.

DURYODHANA: Who is this child who accompanies you?

VYASA: I met him on my way. He never leaves me. I'm telling him your story.

DRAUPADI: Vyasa, have you condemned us to stay all the time in the same place? To watch our life ebb away in this forest?

VYASA: No. Nothing compels you to stagnate here. Go. The forest land is vast. Profit from exile to see and listen. Walk. Pause beside wise men. Question savages and madmen. Listen to stories; it's always pleasant and sometimes it improves you. *To Duryodhana* Duryodhana, go back to the city, today's hunt has not been very good. *The Pandavas collect their few belongings while the Kauravas leave reluctantly. At the last minute, Bhima says to Dushassana:*

BHIMA: Dushassana, do me a favor: as you go back through the forest, be very careful. Keep your throat well away from tigers and wolves. Stay alive. Save your blood for me. *They all leave except Vyasa and the boy who says:*

BOY: If you can stop crimes, you could prevent the war?

VYASA: There are acts that a word can check, others nothing can block.

BOY: And Krishna? Why doesn't he help his friends?

VYASA: He's caught up in a war far from here.

BOY: In a war? He has enemies?

VYASA: Of course.

BOY: Vyasa, I don't want to stay in the forest anymore. I'm afraid. *A moment before, a servant appeared. She prepares a bed. In turn, Gandhari appears. Vyasa says to the child:*

VYASA: You're no longer in the forest.

# THE SEARCH FOR ARMS

*Gandhari leans over a bowl of boiling water, undoing her long hair and passing it through the steam. Suddenly, she raises her head and asks:*

GANDHARI: Who is there? *Kunti has just appeared and says:*

KUNTI: Kunti.

GANDHARI: What do you want?

KUNTI: Uncover your eyes, Gandhari. *Gandhari does not reply, staying on her guard.*

KUNTI: Your son has launched a hunt against my sons. Not satisfied with their exile, he wants their death, he wants to touch their corpses.

GANDHARI: He is defending his kingdom.

KUNTI: Take off your veil, come out of your dark hiding place.

GANDHARI: To each one his darkness, Kunti. I am used to the night.

KUNTI: You never look at the earth, the palace, nor the colors of the sky. That I understand, but how can you live without ever seeing your sons? *Gandhari does not reply.* A spark of courage, that's all you need. Look around you, see things as they are. I'm going to tear off your veil. *Kunti moves to remove the veil and Gandhari pulls back.*

GANDHARI: Don't touch me. *Kunti does not move.*

KUNTI: You don't like me, Gandhari. My first son was born before yours and you haven't forgotten.

GANDHARI: I suffered for a long time, it's true. I even asked myself what fathers could have given you your sons, but I don't think of it anymore. Listen to me, Kunti. Your children are united and they're strong enough to protect themselves. It's for mine that I fear the worst. The rage in Duryodhana's heart makes a weakling of him.

KUNTI: He's a blind man's son. He lives blindly.

GANDHARI: He's his own threat, he's bringing death upon himself. I see it clearly. You must help me to keep him alive. Even if you hate him, even if the earth fears him, he's my son. *Suddenly they stop as Karna has just entered carrying a lance. His secret mother, Kunti, says to him at once:*

KUNTI: Come, Karna. *Karna approaches the two women.* Karna, each day I feel the breath of war come closer. I know your power and your influence. If you wished, you could avert it.

KARNA: It's not me who decides if there'll be a war. But if the day comes, I will fight. Your sons are my enemies. They have despised, soiled, and rejected me.

KUNTI: You can never beat them.

KARNA: You see this lance? Touch it, feel how it vibrates. *He presents the lance to Kunti who touches it lightly.* When I was born, I had a golden breastplate like a second skin that nothing could pierce. One day, a god disguised as a beggar said to me, "Give me your breastplate." I heard a voice in the sky crying, "Don't part with that breastplate." But I couldn't refuse. I can never refuse anything. Without the least hesitation I tore it off and gave it, dripping with blood. It was then that the god held out this lance to me, with these words: "It will kill a living being, whomever you choose—man, god, or demon.

KUNTI: But it will only kill once.

KARNA: How do you know that?

KUNTI: I just know.

KARNA: Kunti, your sons are afraid of me. Duryodhana has given me a kingdom and I owe him my life—more than my life. One day, when the sun is high, I will bring him victory.

KUNTI: If you had brothers, if you had a mother, would you still speak of victory? *Karna is quiet for a moment, then, indicating Gandhari, says:*

KARNA: I have a mother and I have a hundred brothers. Leave us, Kunti. *Kunti is about to leave when Duryodhana comes in with Dushassana. Karna asks him:*

KARNA: Did you see them?

DURYODHANA: Yes, but Arjuna has left the forest.

KARNA: I know. My spies saw him, heading north, alone. *Vyasa reappears and Duryodhana asks him:*

DURYODHANA: Vyasa, where is he going?

VYASA: I sent him to look for weapons.

DURYODHANA: What weapons?

VYASA: Sacred weapons, those that bring all existence to its end.

KARNA: How does he expect to find them?

DURYODHANA: Speak quickly!

VYASA: By penitence, abstinence.

DURYODHANA: Where is he? I must know exactly.

VYASA: I'm unable to tell you. *Karna then says to Duryodhana:*

KARNA: You can see him! Concentrate your thoughts on him, be calm, pronounce the necessary words. Evoke him! *Duryodhana calms down and concentrates. His lips move. Everyone is silent. Duhsa-*

*sana helps him with his preparation. Kunti and Gandhari have stayed. There is music. Time seems to stop. Long lines of fire spring out of the earth. Through the flames, Arjuna appears. Kunti is the first to speak:*

KUNTI: Arjuna!

GANDHARI: Arjuna is here? You see him? Where is he?

DURYODHANA: He is seated in a thorny wood on the back of the Himalayas. He has been there for months, without food, without sleep. *Seeing an animal, Arjuna takes his bow, shoots, and kills it. As he goes to pick it up a voice says:*

HUNTER: Don't touch that boar!

ARJUNA: Who are you? *A man leaps into sight, dressed in furs, carrying a bow. He seems formidable. He says to Arjuna:*

HUNTER: I hunt in these vast mountains. This boar is mine. Why did you shoot it down?

ARJUNA: This boar is mine. I hit it first.

HUNTER: It was I who hit it. Before you! What brings you here alone, in the icy wind? *The hunter moves toward the boar.*

ARJUNA: Don't go near that boar!

HUNTER: I take the boar, I lift it onto my shoulders, it is mine. *Arjuna lifts his bow.*

ARJUNA: If your hand touches the skin of this animal, you won't escape alive.

HUNTER: You can't frighten me. The earth here knows my step. You shot at the boar and you missed. Don't put your clumsiness onto others. I'm taking my boar. *The hunter takes the boar. Arjuna shoots his arrow but the hunter dodges it, laughing. Arjuna shoots a second and third arrow. The hunter avoids them. He mocks Arjuna.*

HUNTER: Again! Again! More! More! Use up all your arrows! You can't touch me! *Gandhari asks Kunti:*

GANDHARI: Arjuna has missed his target?

KARNA: Who called him the finest archer in the world? A simple hunter can avoid his arrows?

DURYODHANA: Who is this laughing man? *Arjuna throws himself onto the hunter and they fight barehanded. But all Arjuna's efforts fail against the hunter's strength and cunning. As the hunter repulses him he says:*

HUNTER: You can do nothing to me. I master you. I block your lungs. You can't breathe. Look, I lift you in my arms. *The hunter, having lifted Arjuna in his arms, lets him go. Arjuna falls senseless to the ground.*

KUNTI: My son isn't breathing anymore. He's lying rigid on the ground.

GANDHARI: Who has brought him down? *Arjuna slowly comes round.*

DURYODHANA: He recovers. He molds a handful of earth into an homage to Shiva. He covers it with a crown of flowers. He turns round. The hunter is there and on his head he wears the same crown of flowers. *Arjuna looks at the hunter and recognizes him.*

ARJUNA: Shiva . . .

KUNTI: Shiva . . .

KARNA: Shiva . . .

DURYODHANA: Shiva . . . *They all bow in front of Shiva. Then Arjuna rises and says to the hunter who now appears as Shiva:*

ARJUNA: Shiva, you, the most subtle of beings, blue-necked Shiva with your third eye, I came to these mountains, drawn by a longing to see you. In this thorny wood on the back of the Himalayas, where I have lived for two years, with ice and wind straining my spirit, I reached the farthest frontier of pain. I fought without recognizing you. I am confused, forgive me.

SHIVA: You are forgiven. I am pleased with you. Ask me a favor, whatever you wish.

ARJUNA: What I wish is an absolute weapon that you possess.

SHIVA: Pasupata?

ARJUNA: Yes.

SHIVA: It can destroy the world.

ARJUNA: I know.

SHIVA: You can launch it with your bow, but also with your eye, your word, your thought. It's a weapon you can't recall. It's without limit, without mercy.

ARJUNA: I know that too.

SHIVA: You could never dispose of it, nor give it back.

ARJUNA: I need this weapon.

SHIVA: I give it to you. *Shiva gives the weapon to Arjuna as Dushassana cries:*

DUSHASSANA: He's giving him Pasupata! *Karna and Duryodhana are silent.*

DUSHASSANA: The mountains quiver when they hear that name. The trees, the wind, the whole earth shakes.

KARNA: Arjuna will never dare use it. He doesn't know how. *Arjuna steps toward Karna and, as Shiva disappears, he says:*

ARJUNA: Karna, you are mistaken. Listen to what happened to me; listen carefully: when Shiva disappeared I heard a tumult in the sky, like a hundred thousand claps of thunder and an immense chariot appeared, scattering the clouds. Flaming air came screaming from the chariot, its blazing mirror-weapons shone unbearably through the dense vapors.

KARNA: Who are you in the form of Arjuna? An apparition? A phantom?

ARJUNA: The voice of the driver said to me, "Mount!" My heart beat wildly, I asked the driver to control his invisible horses, then I bid farewell to the mountain, I said to it: "My eyes have rested on your snow and your streams. I have drunk the clear water flowing from your sides and I have seen the gods draw near. I thank you and I leave." I climbed onto the immense chariot. Drawn by a prodigious force, it bore me to the regions of light, which the earth calls stars. Yes, Karna, I saw thousands of fiery spheres, making music in endless space.

KARNA: You can't frighten me by talking of the sky.

ARJUNA: I saw bodies glowing with their own light. Spirits streaked and dissolved before my eye. I saw Airavata, the enormous white elephant with four tusks. I passed beyond the world of men, I arrived at Amaravati, the indescribable city where Indra, my father, lives. He took me on his knee, yes Karna, he caressed me with his hand, a hand burnt black with tracks of thunder. And for five years with him, I deepened my understanding of the use of this weapon.

KARNA: You don't exist. I don't believe you.

ARJUNA: I will find you again. *As Arjuna moves away, disappearing, Duryodhana says to Karna:*

DURYODHANA: It is night.

KARNA: Yes.

DURYODHANA: You still dread the night?

KARNA: I don't like it. I like the sun, when it wraps me in its warmth, when it scorches me. Every evening, when shadows lengthen, I feel cold, I look behind me, I sleep badly. But when the first rays touch me, my strength returns intact, the sun kills night's terrors and darkness takes flight.

DURYODHANA: Karna, you have often promised me victory—total victory. This limitless weapon, Pasupata; you, too, must acquire it, whatever the cost. Otherwise, what good is your promise?

KARNA: We will have it.

*At this moment a woman (Urvasi) runs in lightly. Duryodhana and Karna look at her. She stops and calls:*

URVASI: Arjuna! *Arjuna reappears.*

ARJUNA: Who are you?

URVASI: My name is Urvasi. I am an Apsaras. I dwell in the rivers of paradise.

ARJUNA: What do you want of me?

URVASI: Indra, your father, sent me word: "My son Arjuna is here, but he is alone, without a woman for five years. Prepare to go to his room this evening." I circled my eyes with shadow and my arms with gold; I scented my skin. I drank a little wine. I came rapidly through the gardens.

ARJUNA: I admire you, Urvasi. Beauty is your shadow.

URVASI: One day you looked me long and straight in the eyes. You made me love you.

ARJUNA: But you are an Apsaras. I am a man.

URVASI: We Apsarasas are free to choose; we are not tied to a husband. What I offer you is neither frightening, nor dangerous. It is only love.

ARJUNA: I am too far from the earth. I have forgotten pleasure's shape, even her scent. . . .

URVASI: Love is the same in all the worlds.

ARJUNA: Go away Urvasi. We cannot love each other.

URVASI: I came to you, don't reject me. I love you.

ARJUNA: I love you too and I respect you, like a mother. I bow to you. Treat me as your son.

URVASI: Look at my skin. It is seething with fury. Treat you as my son! Remember my words: because you have insulted a woman who came to love you, you will live like a woman, you too, amongst women. You will be despised and you will be deprived of your virility. *Urvasi leaves quickly. Karna speaks directly to Arjuna:*

KARNA: Why did you reject her? Did she frighten you? Have you lost your manhood in the sky? *Arjuna looks at Karna then leaves without replying. Duryodhana says to Karna:*

DURYODHANA: What is this new mystery? Why this lost virility? She did not say for how long.

KARNA: That's the moment to attack him, when he's like a woman.

GANDHARI: Stop talking of your manhood, your weapons, your wars!

DURYODHANA: Our enemies are consolidating their positions; they threaten us. We can't wait like children, unprotected. Vyasa! *Vyasa, who had disappeared, reappears at once with the boy.*

VYASA: I am here.

DURYODHANA: Vyasa, I need to know. Arjuna, when he came back from the sky, did he find his brothers again?

VYASA: Yes.

DURYODHANA: Tell me, what lands did they visit? What did they see? What did they hear?

VYASA: Their walk was long, their adventures magnificent, and the secrets they learned were infinite. They even experienced death.

DURYODHANA: Death? *At this point Nakula and Sahadeva appear. They seem exhausted and are going toward a lake. As they are about to drink, a voice (Vyasa's disguised voice) says to them:*

VOICE: No! Don't drink! Answer my questions before drinking!

NAKULA: Where did that voice come from? *They look all around. No one answers. The twins lean once more toward the lake.*

VOICE: Don't drink! First, answer my questions!

NAKULA: I'm parched with thirst. I must drink. *The twins lean over, drink, and fall down dead. Duryodhana and Dushassana watch in astonishment. They move away as they see Arjuna appear. Arjuna goes to the twins' motionless bodies.*

ARJUNA: The sons of Madri are dead. Who has killed them? *Suddenly he seems to be seized by thirst and leans over to drink from the lake.*

VOICE: Why are you so avid for water? Answer my questions before you drink! *Arjuna straightens up and shoots arrows in all directions.*

ARJUNA: Where's this invisible enemy hiding? Show yourself!

VOICE: Don't excite yourself for nothing. First answer my questions.

ARJUNA: No! I'm devoured by a thirst I can't explain. *Arjuna drinks and falls down, dead.*
   *Bhima then arrives carrying his heavy club. He sees his brothers' bodies.*

BHIMA: Who has killed my brothers? What terrible battle is waiting for me? Where does this thirst come from? *In turn, he leans toward the lake.*

VOICE: Don't drink! First answer my questions!

BHIMA: The thirst is too strong. I must drink. *He drinks and falls down, dead. Then Yudhishthira appears. He goes to his brothers' bodies and looks at them in anguish.*

YUDHISHTHIRA: Who has struck them down? I see no trace of blows. I don't understand. A brutal thirst grabs me by the throat. . . . *He bends toward the lake. The voice comes:*

VOICE: First, answer my questions. Then I'll let you drink. *Yudhishthira looks in every direction.*

YUDHISHTHIRA: Who are you? I don't see you! Are you in the water? Are you in the air?

VOICE: I am neither fish, nor bird. I struck down your brothers because they wanted to drink without answering my questions. *Yudhishthira does not move, overcoming his thirst.*

YUDHISHTHIRA: Examine me.

VOICE: What is quicker than the wind?

YUDHISHTHIRA: Thought.

VOICE: What can cover the earth?

YUDHISHTHIRA: Darkness.

VOICE: Who are the more numerous, the living or the dead?

YUDHISHTHIRA: The living, because the dead are no longer.

VOICE: Give me an example of space.

YUDHISHTHIRA: My two hands as one.

VOICE: An example of grief.

YUDHISHTHIRA: Ignorance.

VOICE: Of poison.

YUDHISHTHIRA: Desire.

VOICE: An example of defeat.

YUDHISHTHIRA: Victory.

VOICE: Which animal is the slyest?

YUDHISHTHIRA: The one that man does not yet know.

VOICE: Which came first, day or night?

YUDHISHTHIRA: Day, but it was only a day ahead.

VOICE: What is the cause of the world?

YUDHISHTHIRA: Love.

VOICE: What is your opposite?

YUDHISHTHIRA: Myself.

VOICE: What is madness?

YUDHISHTHIRA: A forgotten way.

VOICE: And revolt? Why do men revolt?

YUDHISHTHIRA: To find beauty, either in life or in death.

VOICE: What for each of us is inevitable?

YUDHISHTHIRA: Happiness.

VOICE: And what is the greatest wonder?

YUDHISHTHIRA: Each day, death strikes and we live as though we were immortal. This is the greatest wonder. *Vyasa returns among them.*

VYASA: Then the voice from the lake said: "May all your brothers come back to life, for I am Dharma, your father. I am rightness, constancy, the order of the world. *The dead brothers rise. Draupadi comes to join them.* The wish to know you drew me here. Yudhishthira, I am very satisfied." And Dharma added, "Choose a favor."

YUDHISHTHIRA: Our stay in the woods is coming to an end. We must now spend a thirteenth year unseen, unrecognized. Tell me what our disguise should be.

VYASA: Dharma answered him: "Choose the disguise of your most secret desires."

YUDHISHTHIRA: Where can we hide?

VYASA: For the thirteenth year, you must hide so skillfully that no one could recognize you, not even me. *The Pandavas and Draupadi leave, as do Kunti and Gandhari.*

DURYODHANA: Karna, too many enigmas surround me. I'm losing all my confidence. I will send thousands of spies to the corners of the world to find them, but I must have this absolute weapon—Pasupata—very quickly. I must have it.

KARNA: I leave at once.

DUSHASSANA: Do you know where to find it?

KARNA: Yes, I know. Dushassana, stop trembling for your life.

DURYODHANA: Karna, I am naked, threatened. Don't disappoint me. *The three men leave. Vyasa stays with the boy who says to him:*

BOY: I'm afraid of Pasupata.

VYASA: So am I.

BOY: Do you think Karna will succeed?

VYASA: There's nothing he can't do. Come.

BOY: Vyasa, why are you inventing this poem?

VYASA: So as to engrave dharma in the hearts of men.

BOY: Is that possible?

VYASA: It will be long and difficult. It will even be dangerous. But the earth is listening to my poem. It's wondering: will he find a way to help me? *They start walking.*

BOY: Where are we going?

VYASA: I don't know yet.

BOY: Are you really the author of this poem?

VYASA: Do you doubt it?

BOY: At times you hesitate. I get the feeling you don't know anything anymore.

VYASA: I've composed everything, but nothing is written down. Yes, there are moments when my thoughts escape me.

BOY: And Krishna? Did you invent him as well? *Krishna appears.*

KRISHNA: Vyasa, which of us has invented the other?

BOY: Krishna . . .

VYASA: Greetings. What are you looking for in this land?

KRISHNA: Vyasa, I was looking for you. I'm troubled.

BOY: You?

KRISHNA: I'm a little cold. *The boy puts a blanket around Krishna's shoulders.*

VYASA: What's troubling you?

KRISHNA: At times, I am calm. I feel traversed by a luminous force and everything seems clear. Then a man runs up to me, bleeding. He is afraid; he tells of cries, of massacres. He says: "Everyone wants your death." I have to brace myself, stamp out all that rises against me and I wonder: why this chaos, why these tears?

VYASA: You expect me to reply?

KRISHNA: Perhaps.

BOY: Who are you? People say Vishnu has come down to save the world and some say he has taken your shape. Is it true?

KRISHNA: What would you say, Vyasa? *Vyasa replies with a vague gesture.*

KRISHNA: You who are narrating me, haven't you already traced out my path?

VYASA: No path is traced completely, as well you know. You are in life and you live.

KRISHNA: The days of my youth passed joyfully and I tasted many wonders.

VYASA: Now your hairs go gray and all is in question.

KRISHNA: Deep in myself I see a black lake. Often in the dark I hear calling and cries of pain.

VYASA: I hear them too.

KRISHNA: And what do you do?

VYASA: At night, I sleep, and in the morning I wake. I wait.

BOY: But you must know what is being prepared? One of you must know? *Terrible but human cries are heard, startling Vyasa, Krishna, and the boy. The cries are chilling.*

BOY: Who's shouting?

KRISHNA: Quick. Hide. It's Parashurama. *All three hide.*
    *A ghastly person appears; a hermit covered in ashes. His furious cries*

*are threatening invocations. A modestly clad servant, who is not instantly recognizable, follows at a distance. He is carrying an axe and a cloth. The boy asks Krishna:*

BOY: Who is it?

KRISHNA: An extraordinary hermit, as powerful as time. The man with the axe.

BOY: Look at his servant. He's another Karna.

KRISHNA: It is Karna.

BOY: He's disguised as well?

VYASA: Silence. *The boy is quiet.*
   *Parashurama calms down; he sits. Karna, his servant, comes toward him in a servile manner and puts the axe on the ground. He then wipes Parashurama's face and body with a cloth he is holding.*

PARASHURAMA: For many months you have lived in these forests, silent and willing. You have prepared my rice, you have watched over my sleep, you have washed my body. I want to grant you a favor. Tell me your desire. *Karna remains silent, humble.* I don't know the color of your eyes, for you have never raised them to me. I don't know the sound of your voice, I don't know your name, but I tell you, you deserve a reward and I have many well-hidden secrets. What is your wish?

KARNA: Pasupata . . .

PARASHURAMA: What?

KARNA: Give me the secret of Pasupata. . . . *A moment's silence, then the hermit shouts threateningly:*

PARASHURAMA: Who are you?

KARNA: I am your servant.

PARASHURAMA: Liar. You want a weapon—that means you are a warrior. You belong to that arrogant caste that I detest, the Kshatriyas!

KARNA: Why do you detest them? *The hermit stands up brandishing the axe.*

PARASHURAMA: There's nothing to explain. I hate them. I felled twenty-one generations of Kshatriyas with my axe. I came down from heaven to destroy them.

KARNA: I'm not of that caste. I'm a simple man.

PARASHURAMA: That's the truth?

KARNA: I'm called the driver's son. I swear it. *Parashurama thinks for a moment, then hands Karna a piece of bark that he has just picked up from the ground.*

PARASHURAMA: Here, I'm a man of my word. The formula's written here. Learn it by heart. *Karna reads the piece of bark.* Quick! Hurry! *Karna reads very carefully.* The formula will fade away. Finished. It's only a scrap of bark. You remember what was on it? *Karna nods. Parashurama throws away the piece of bark.* When you utter those words, a creature will come down from the sky and will give you the weapon that you wish. *The hermit yawns and stretches.* Now I will sleep a little. I'm more than a thousand years old and I'm beginning to grow tired. *He lies down, putting his head in Karna's lap, and goes to sleep. Karna stays motionless.*

*A worm approaches Karna and bites his thigh. Karna's suffering is terrible, but he does not move, he does not complain.*

*The hermit wakes. He sees blood on his hand and, very annoyed, asks Karna:* Where does this blood come from? Is this your doing?

KARNA: A worm bored a hole in my thigh while you slept, a tiny worm. Forgive me.

PARASHURAMA: Why didn't you yell?

KARNA: I didn't want to wake you. *Parashurama grabs the axe and threatens Karna.*

PARASHURAMA: You have tricked me. Only a Kshatriya could display such idiotic courage. Any intelligent man would have yelled. You're a Kshatriya. You lied to worm out my secret, but listen to me, whoever you are: at the last minute—listen to me carefully—the secret will slip from your memory, you will forget it entirely and that will be the moment of your death. *Karna wishes to speak, but the hermit prevents him, brandishing the axe.* Go! *Karna leaves rapidly.*

*Parashurama then addresses Vyasa and Krishna without looking at them:* Krishna, I saw you. And you too, Vyasa. Don't hide from me. The whole world is putting on masks. You too. Don't stay naked. Farewell. *Parashurama goes.*

# THE COURT OF KING VIRATA

*The forest has vanished. The scene has changed; there is an atmosphere of Oriental grace and charm. A king, Virata, enters with members of his court, musicians, and servants. He consults a tablet he is carrying and asks:*

VIRATA: Where's my head attendant?

HEAD ATTENDANT: Your head attendant's here.

VIRATA: What's this I read on my block? Five new servants! Whatever for? My servants already stretch from here to the ocean. Why make a river with my gold?

HEAD ATTENDANT: These five men, O great Virata, seem to my poor eyes superior to all those who have served you up to now.

VIRATA: Truly?

HEAD ATTENDANT: Truly. That's why I engaged them. Would you like to see for yourself?

VIRATA: Yes. Let the first one in. What's his name? Kanka? *The head attendant claps his hands and calls:*

HEAD ATTENDANT: Kanka! *Yudhishthira enters dressed as a brahmin.*

VIRATA: Who are you?

YUDHISHTHIRA: I am a brahmin, cast down by fate, led to your doors by desperate need. My name is Kanka. In better times, Yudhishthira was my friend. With him I wandered far and wide, we visited seven hundred holy places and I could tell you sixteen thousand essential fables. Besides, I play at dice.

VIRATA: You play at dice?

YUDHISHTHIRA: Yes, in the course of my journeys a wise man taught me the science of dice and I can pass it on. If you follow my advice you will never lose.

VIRATA: Never?

YUDHISHTHIRA: I told you, never. *Virata, delighted, claps his hands and calls:*

VIRATA: Uttara, come here. Come, my son. *To Yudhishthira* Good players are always my friends.

YUDHISHTHIRA: I know. *A young man has just appeared.*

VIRATA: This is my son, Uttara, the light of my life, handsome as the sun, brave as a lion. Take him in hand. *Uttara bows to the false brahmin. Virata returns to his block:* And this one? Balhava? Who is he?

HEAD ATTENDANT: A colossus, a mountain of strength, a walking volcano. This morning he passed the time lifting horses in the court-yard.

VIRATA: He lifted horses? All by himself?

HEAD ATTENDANT: All by himself.

VIRATA: With his hands?

HEAD ATTENDANT: With one hand.

VIRATA: I want to see him! *The head attendant claps and calls:*

HEAD ATTENDANT: Balhava! *Bhima enters.*

VIRATA: Who are you?

BHIMA: I'm Balhava, the cook, the terrible cutthroat of sheep, the master of four thousand sauces. In the past I worked for King Yudhishthira, who set me above all his other cooks. He called me the prince of pots.

VIRATA: I've a weakness for good cooking. As of tonight, I want to taste one of your dishes. *At this moment a new character enters, a general called Kichaka. He is vain, ostentatious, and agitated.*

VIRATA: What is it, Kichaka? You're in a terrible state. What's on your mind?

KICHAKA: The Pandavas have disappeared!

VIRATA: Well?

KICHAKA: Duryodhana is furious. His spies are scouring the earth for them. If I find them, he will give me gold.

YUDHISHTHIRA: I think you should search in remote hamlets.

KICHAKA: Yes.

BHIMA: In faraway mines, caves . . . grottoes . . .

KICHAKA: Yes. I will track them down, even if it takes me to China. Who are these men?

VIRATA: My new servants. They served Yudhishthira in the forest.

KICHAKA: Yudhishthira? *To Bhima* Where is he now?

BHIMA: No one knows. Perhaps he died from shame.

VIRATA: What else? A groom? *The twins are introduced.*

NAKULA: I know all the desires and secrets of cows.

VIRATA: The secrets of cows? Very good. And who else? A musician? Good. I'll take them all. What do I see? A eunuch? I've already got too many eunuchs. I've more eunuchs than wives. *The head attendant claps and Arjuna enters completely transformed, dressed as a woman, wearing bracelets and earrings, accompanied by music. His bearing and mannerisms are very effeminate.*

VIRATA: Who are you?

ARJUNA: My name is Vrihannala. I teach music, dancing, singing. I was leading dancer to a queen.

VIRATA: Are you a man or a woman?

ARJUNA: I am a man and a woman. I kept guard over the harem for the great King Yudhishthira and now I sing wherever I'm allowed to sing.

VIRATA: Then you can teach music to my wife and daughter.

ARJUNA: O great king Virata, I am very satisfied. Your wives have nothing to fear from me.

VIRATA: So I see. *Very suspicious, Kichaka counts the five new musicians.*

KICHAKA: One, two, three, four, five. They are five like the Pandavas! *To Bhima* Come! *Bhima approaches. Kichaka feels his muscles.* This one is very strong. *To Yudhishthira* And this one ... What have you got in your hand? *Yudhishthira opens his hand.*

YUDHISHTHIRA: Dice.

KICHAKA: You play at dice?

YUDHISHTHIRA: Yes, very often.

KICHAKA: So tell me: you win or you lose?

NAKULA: He wins every time.

KICHAKA: Then you can't be Yudhishthira. *The five brothers breathe again.*

 *Kichaka stops abruptly in front of Draupadi who has just come in. She is very poorly clad. Gudeshna, Virata's wife, introduces her:*

GUDESHNA: I met this woman in front of the palace. She told me she's called Sairindhri and she's looking for work.

VIRATA: Indeed! I've already enough servants to make a women's army! Why still one more?

GUDESHNA: Look at her. Look what a noble head rises from her shabby clothes! How she holds herself! And what force is in her gaze! *Virata looks closely at Draupadi.*

VIRATA: You are absolutely right. Who are you?

GUDESHNA: She won't answer you. To me, a woman, she said this: "I am only a servant. I know how to plait hair, blend perfumes. I served Queen Draupadi. I went in the forest with her and now I go where the wind blows." *Since Draupadi's entrance, Kichaka is as though hypnotised by her.*

KICHAKA: If you don't want this woman, give her to me. I will take her for my house.

VIRATA: I never said I didn't want her, though this woman frightens me, for beauty is always a danger.

BHIMA: Who wouldn't lose his mind for her? Even the trees bow down when she passes.

KICHAKA: You know her?

BHIMA: No, I was just thinking out loud.

UTTARA: You who know Yudhishthira and his brothers, tell. . . .

VIRATA: Yes. Tell us. We've heard so many travelers' tales.

UTTARA: Is it true that Bhima met Hanuman?

YUDHISHTHIRA: Yes, it's true.

UTTARA: Hanuman? The miraculous monkey?

VIRATA: How did it happen? Kanka, do you know?

YUDHISHTHIRA: Yes, I know. It was because of Draupadi. Bhima loved her more than all in the world. He would have done anything for her. One day, the northeast wind brought with it a thousand-petaled lotus, the very image of the sun. Draupadi picked it up and showed it to Bhima saying, "Look at this heavenly flower, this rarest of flowers. Go, for love of me, gather me a bouquet."

NAKULA: So Bhima turned his face toward the wind and set off carrying his bow and his arrows. He crossed plains and mountains in all his magnificence, full of joy, making the ground thunder with his stride. He breathed the scent of flowers wafted toward him by his father, the wind. He saw birds whose wings glistened with moisture, and following them he found himself beside a lake. He plunged into it, swam for a long while in the clear water, clambered up the opposite shore, and blew his conch. *Arjuna, still in woman's clothing, intervenes:*

ARJUNA: This sound reached the ears of Hanuman, his brother, who was dozing amongst the banana leaves. Hanuman said to himself: "My brother is approaching me on the road to heaven, he mustn't go any farther." So he laid down on the ground and put his tail—his long, hairy tail—across the path. *When Bhima tries to pass, Arjuna, laying a belt or stick on the ground, says to him:*

ARJUNA–HANUMAN: Who are you? Where are you going? We who have animals for mothers don't know too well what is right and what isn't. But you, a man, blessed with reason, why have you come so far? This road is forbidden to humans. Turn back! *Bhima in turn joins the narrative.*

BHIMA: "Who am I?" Bhima answered, taking him for an ordinary monkey. "I am Bhima, son of Kunti and son of the wind. Let me pass! Out of my way!"

ARJUNA–HANUMAN: I can't stand. I'm ill. Very ill. If you really want to pass, jump over my body.

BHIMA: No, I won't jump over the body of a monkey. My own brother is a monkey, the splendid Hanuman, the most powerful of monkeys. He crossed the sea with a single leap. I'm like him. Strength is in our family. Stand up or I'll catapult you to your death.

ARJUNA–HANUMAN: Forgive me. I am old and I cannot get up. Lift this tail which is across your path and pass. *Bhima continues, combining actions with words:*

BHIMA: Bhima took the monkey's tail in his left hand; he pulled but he could not lift it. He seized it with his right hand; he pulled but he could not lift it. He braced himself, took a deep breath, clenched his teeth, wrinkled his forehead till it gleamed with sweat, but he couldn't lift that tail. So he dropped to his knees before the monkey and said to him: "Forgive me. Who are you in the shape of a monkey? If it's not one of heaven's secrets, tell me."

ARJUNA–HANUMAN: I am your brother, Hanuman. This path must not be used by mortals, that's why I stopped you.

BHIMA: You are Hanuman?

ARJUNA–HANUMAN: Yes, have no doubt.

BHIMA: This meeting fills me with joy, son of my father. But there's a special favor I'd like to ask you: let me see you in your other form, in all its gigantic, incomparable, sacred splendor.

ARJUNA–HANUMAN: "No one can see that form," replied Hanuman in his deep and gentle voice. "In the older days, yes, mortals could contemplate it, but this age is the age of destruction. The earth, the trees, man, gods all follow the movement of the times. Bodies die, spirits die, even forms die. My form is dead."

VIRATA: He said that? He said, we are living in the age of destruction? *Yudhishthira takes up the story:*

YUDHISHTHIRA: And this is what he added: "I see the coming of another age, where barbaric kings rule over a vicious, broken world; where puny, fearful, hard men live tiny lives, white hair at sixteen, copulating with animals, their women perfect whores, making love with greedy mouths. The cows dry, sterile; trees stunted, lifeless; no more flowers, no more purity; ambition, corruption, commerce, its the age of Kali, the black time. The countryside a desert, crime stalks the cities, beasts drink blood and sleep in the streets, all the waters sucked up by the sky, scalded earth scorched to dead ash. The fire rises borne by the wind, fire pierces the earth, cracks open the underground world, wind and fire calcinate the world, immense clouds gather—blue, yellow, and red—they rise like deep-sea monsters, like shattered cities. Forked with lightning, the rains fall, the rains fall and engulf the earth; twelve years of storm, the mountains split the waters, I no longer see the world. Then the primary god—when all that remains is a gray sea, without man, beast, or tree—the creator, drinks the terrible wind and falls asleep." *They stay silent for a moment, then the young prince asks:*

UTTARA: And what did Bhima do?

BHIMA: Bhima said to Hanuman: "I am stubborn, I won't go without seeing your ancient shape!" So the monkey, smiling, to please his brother, began to grow bigger, and bigger. His chin rose above the clouds, his eyes became red suns, his teeth gleamed like glaciers. He rose to his full height, enormous, filling all the corners of infinite space. Bhima, stupefied, said to him: "Come down. Stop. That's enough! Become yourself again! I can't look at you anymore!"

ARJUNA: Hanuman became a monkey once more and said to his brother, "Go on your way to the lotus flowers. Gather them gently;

be humble and patient. I love you, may this kiss wipe away your fatigue." *They embrace.*

NAKULA: Bhima set off again, he found a lake covered with thousand-petaled lotuses and returned to Draupadi with her bouquet.

VIRATA: I'm delighted with your story, but it's time to sleep. May your night be rich in dreams. *They all leave except Kichaka, who detains the queen, and indicating Draupadi, asks:*

KICHAKA: Who's this beauty? What's the story?

GUDESHNA: I don't know. I met her in the street.

KICHAKA: I beseech you, beloved sister, send her to me. Think of a way. I must have her. I'll give you emeralds.

GUDESHNA: Return to your palace. *Kichaka leaves at once.* Sairindhri!

DRAUPADI: Your Majesty?

GUDESHNA: Go to Kichaka. He is preparing me a special drink. Bring it to me.

DRAUPADI: I beg you, send another servant.

GUDESHNA: Why?

DRAUPADI: I see lust in his eyes. He's drunk with pride. He'll stop at nothing and I'm married, Majesty.

GUDESHNA: You?

DRAUPADI: A powerful husband protects me. Something terrible could happen to your brother.

GUDESHNA: Take this jug. Do as I say. *The queen leaves.*

*At his palace Kichaka awaits Draupadi. He is very excited and calls a musician to him:*

KICHAKA: Quick! Bring flowers, jewels, silken robes! Prepare a couch, the ivory couch! *Draupadi arrives. Kichaka greets her with flowers and a song. He then dismisses the musician and says:* Come, give me your hand, come. . . .

DRAUPADI: The queen sent me to fetch . . .

KICHAKA: Sit down, sit down. . . . From now on, all my wives are your servants. Ah, there's no one like you. You shine like the moon, your two breasts, your lips, the way your dress folds at the waist, hiding the door to the cavern in your secret forest of love. . . . Sit down, come! *He tries to draw her to his couch.*

DRAUPADI: I'm nobody. I dress hair and I'm another man's wife.

KICHAKA: Don't push me away. You'll regret it. Virata is feeble, he depends on me. I'm in charge of everything. Come!

DRAUPADI: You're sick. I already see you in ashes.

KICHAKA: In ashes? Just the reverse! I'll burn you with love, like a dragon. Come, come into my fire.

DRAUPADI: You're just a stupid child who thinks he can walk on a river.

KICHAKA: And who do you think you are to say no to me? Come, open your arms and close your mouth. *He seizes a weapon and threatens her. King Virata appears and commands:*

VIRATA: Kichaka, let that woman go! Come and play dice!

KICHAKA: This servant resisted me! She threatened me!

VIRATA: A game will calm you down. Come! *Kichaka leaves reluctantly. Draupadi flees.*
   *Meanwhile, Bhima is asleep in his room. Draupadi enters and goes up to him in the shadows.*

DRAUPADI: Bhima? It's me. . . . You're asleep? *He has difficulty in waking up.* How can you sleep? Wake up, Bhima! *Bhima wakes and takes her in his arms.*

BHIMA: Draupadi, you're pale. What is it? Tell me quickly before anyone sees us.

DRAUPADI: I don't care anymore. I'm alone, lost. I think your brothers are dead.

BHIMA: What do you mean?

DRAUPADI: Your elder brother only lives for his dice. He once nourished the earth and now he eats from a stranger's hand. *She looks tenderly at Bhima and adds:* And you, chopping cabbage in the kitchen. . . . And Arjuna, hidden like a fire at the bottom of a well! The great conqueror teaching a king's daughter to dance! Yes, I'm sad, I'm ashamed. I can't sleep anymore. Look at this miserable dress, these chapped hands. I know some people are beginning to suspect us, but I'm in agony, my heart's racing, listen to it. . . . *She draws Bhima's head to her breast.* I can still feel Kichaka's violence burning me. He'll attack again, I'm sure, but I'd sooner swallow poison than fall into his hands. *Bhima, very moved, says:*

BHIMA: You know the new dance hall?

DRAUPADI: Yes.

BHIMA: Tell Kichaka that he has won you, that you will wait for him there tomorrow when night approaches, alone. . . . *Draupadi hugs him and leaves. Bhima stretches out and conceals himself under a sheet.*

  *Kichaka enters the empty dance hall cautiously. He is magnificently dressed. As he enters, he calls:*

KICHAKA: Sairindhri? Are you there? *Not receiving any reply, he moves forward trying to find his way in the dark.* I received your message, night approaches, I am here. *He bumps into the form lying on the floor wrapped in a sheet. He smiles.* You see, I've spent hours dressing and scenting myself for you. It's a very expensive scent. . . . *He lifts the sheet and slides gently down beside Bhima.* When I left, all my servants gasped, they said I was the king of beauty. Ah, I'm happy. . . . It's like a dream. . . . My feet don't touch the ground. . . . I'm in ecstasy. Yes, yes, caress me, I see you know the ancient art . . . again! *His whole body trembles.* I've never been caressed so strongly! My whole body's tingling. *He slides completely under the sheet.* It's jangling! Speak to me, tell me something! *Bhima's voice is heard saying:*

BHIMA: It's true, you are the king. *Kichaka reappears abruptly, alarmed.*

KICHAKA: What?

BHIMA: It's true, you are the king of beauty. No wonder women adore you.

KICHAKA: What's this voice? *Kichaka tries to stand up and flee. The effort is wasted. Bhima takes him in his arms and suffocates him. Kichaka utters his last cries.*

BHIMA: I take you in my arms now. Yes, I seize your hair, crushing the delightful spray of flowers. You didn't know, did you, that you came here looking for death. My fingers sink into your flesh. I feel your bones snapping with pleasure. I will grind you to powder, my love. *Bhima crushes Kichaka, who stops screaming as Bhima reduces him to a pulp. Then Bhima runs away.*

*Two men appear and stare in amazement at the heap on the floor. They are Kichaka's brothers. They turn the ball over in all directions.*

KICHAKA'S BROTHER: What's this? Is it Kichaka, our brother? These are certainly his clothes, and his perfume. . . . But where's his neck? Where are his feet? Where's his head? Who turned him into a ball? *They leave pushing the ball which rolls out in front of them.*

# THE WAR OF THE COWS

*Members of the court are gathering. A messenger runs in calling:*

MESSENGER: Alas, Majesty, alas, Majesty! *The King appears with his courtiers.*

VIRATA: Well, what is it?

MESSENGER: Spare me, Great King! I have a mother, two wives and several children! Grant me my life!

VIRATA: What do you want?

MESSENGER: Spare me, I bring bad news. Your lands have been invaded, your crops carted away.

VIRATA: What are you saying?

MESSENGER: They have taken your cows! Your thirty thousand cows!

VIRATA: They've taken my cows! Quick! Muster my elephants, my chariots, all my warriors! Let war ring through my kingdom! They've taken my cows! My thirty thousand cows! So who will command my armies? Since the terrible Kichaka was ground into dust by a demon, I've nobody! Where's my son?

UTTARA: Here. *Uttara comes forward rather timidly.*

VIRATA: You are my true blood, you are strength and daring incarnate. Take command of my troops and bring back the cattle.

UTTARA: Me in command?

VIRATA: One day or other a man must fight. The day has come.

UTTARA: Yes, father, I will fight. I would fight with heart and soul if I had a driver for my chariot.

VIRATA: You haven't a driver?

UTTARA: He's ill. I need an expert at handling horses. I can't see anyone. If you find me a good chariot driver, I'll bring back the cows. *At this point, Draupadi starts talking despite Yudhishthira's signals to her to keep quiet.*

DRAUPADI: I know an excellent driver.

VIRATA: Ah?

DRAUPADI: There's no one like him. He can make horses fly like the wind, twist like snakes, and stop dead in their tracks. He used to be the Pandavas' driver.

UTTARA: Who is he? *Draupadi points to Arjuna.*

DRAUPADI: Him. *Everyone seems stunned, including Arjuna.*

ARJUNA: Me?

VIRATA: A singer? A eunuch?

DRAUPADI: There's no one in the world to touch him. If he's your driver, you're sure to win.

UTTARA: But he's a half-and-half. You've only to look. She's trembling. She's scared to death. *He scares Arjuna, who does seem easily frightened, and says to his father:* No, you can't send me to war with *that!*

DRAUPADI: I said what I know.

ARJUNA: How could I ever drive a chariot? How could I hold the reins? I'm terrified of horses.

DRAUPADI: He's lying. He was Arjuna's driver. *Everyone is silent.*

UTTARA: Arjuna's driver?

DRAUPADI: Yes, they were inseparable. You never saw one without the other.

UTTARA: Then agree to drive for me. Arjuna is my idol. Come, let the women giggle. Bring him a breastplate and some weapons!

ARJUNA: A breastplate? Weapons? For me? *Someone hands him a breastplate. He puts it down and tries to put it on feet first. He falls over. Everyone laughs, the women in particular. He is given a sword. He takes it by the blade and drops it. Then bow; he handles it awkwardly, pointing the arrows toward himself, then toward the others. They fling themselves on the ground in mock terror as though trying to protect themselves:* A sword? What can you do with a sword? A bow? Arrows? I've never held a bow in my life! A battle? Blood? Sweat? Dirt? What horror!

UTTARA: Were you Arjuna's driver, yes or no?

ARJUNA: Yes, but since then, I . . .

VIRATA: It's settled. You'll be my son's driver.

UTTARA: And we'll bring you victory.

GUDESHNA: *Laughing, to Arjuna* Don't forget, when you return in triumph, to bring us back some pretty materials.

VIRATA: Off you go! *Uttara and Arjuna go off together. Everyone leaves except Nakula and Draupadi.*

NAKULA: The thirteenth year is not yet over. Why did you push him into the battle?

DRAUPADI: Do you know who's behind this attack? Duryodhana, with Karna.

NAKULA: You're giving them a good pretext for refusing us the kingdom. Draupadi, are you only interested in war?

DRAUPADI: Yes, Nakula, the war has already begun. I won't go back with my head bowed and my tongue tied. I swore I'd never forget. And you'll see all water drain from the earth and all color from the sky before my word loses its power.

# ON THE BATTLEFIELD

*Uttara and Arjuna, advancing on the battlefield, suddenly stop at the sight of the Kauravas and the young Uttara takes fright.*

UTTARA: What do I see? Duryodhana, Drona, Bhishma himself! And Karna! Vrihannala, stop, stop!

ARJUNA: You told me to be your driver. I'm driving.

UTTARA: But it's me alone against this immense army! Alone with a eunuch! I can't! Stop!

ARJUNA: You bragged and boasted in front of the women. If you turn back, they'll die of laughter.

UTTARA: Stop! Let them keep the cows! So I'm ridiculous, I don't care. I'm scared. I want to go home! *The young prince flees, terrified. Arjuna follows him. The Kauravas watch the scene in astonishment.*

DURYODHANA: Who's that, over there, running?

DRONA: It's Uttara, Virata's son.

DURYODHANA: Yes, but behind him, in a long dress?

KARNA: Is it a man or a woman?

DRONA: I'd say a woman.

DUSHASSANA: Why's she running after the boy?

KARNA: Oddly enough, she's got something of Arjuna.

DURYODHANA: Arjuna?

KARNA: Look at her back, look at the arm muscles.

DUSHASSANA: Arjuna dressed as a woman?

KARNA: Who else would dare approach us?

DURYODHANA: Arjuna here? No, it's not him.

DRONA: The woman's running quickly, she's caught up with the king's son. *Arjuna has caught up with Uttara and is holding him back carefully. Uttara says to him, out of breath:*

UTTARA: I'll give you embroidery, rings, necklaces, but leave me, let me go. It's sheer madness.

ARJUNA: Listen to me. You'll drive the chariot now and I'll do the fighting.

UTTARA: You? Fight?

ARJUNA: Yes, me. Arjuna.

UTTARA: You are Arjuna?

ARJUNA: Yes. You've nothing to fear. Come.

UTTARA: You're Arjuna?

ARJUNA: Stop goggling. Take the reins and don't tremble. *The Kauravas see the two men advance.*

KARNA: Yes, it's Arjuna, it's him!

DURYODHANA: The thirteenth year isn't yet up and he dares to face us. He's come out of hiding! He and his brothers must do another twelve years in the forest; they haven't observed the pact. That's true, isn't it, Bhishma?

BHISHMA: If Arjuna shows himself, he knows what he is doing.

DURYODHANA: Answer me directly. Have they respected or rejected the pact?

BHISHMA: It's hard to know the true nature of things. Books of ethics often give us fresh illusions.

DURYODHANA: Answer me!

BHISHMA: And the worst of these illusions—as the wise well know—is war.

DUSHASSANA: What's the use of wise men? They tell long tales in cool palaces, but here in the heat of battle, what can they bring?

BHISHMA: *To Duryodhana* I'm sorry I came with you. One doesn't fight over cows.

DURYODHANA: Answer me clearly for once: is the thirteenth year over, yes or no?

KARNA: *To Duryodhana* Let me fight Arjuna, me alone! *Bhishma turns away.*

DURYODHANA: You're leaving?

BHISHMA: I won't take any part in this battle.

DRONA: Nor will I. *Bhishma and Drona leave. At that moment the sound of Arjuna's bow can be heard.*

DURYODHANA: It's the sound of his bow.

KARNA: Yes, it's Gandiva.

DURYODHANA: Let's fight.

# THE MASKS FALL

*Virata, members of his court, and Yudhishthira await news of the battle.*

VIRATA: Wasn't I mad to let him go?

YUDHISHTHIRA: No, have no fear. He has Vrihannala as driver, he'll bring back the cows.

VIRATA: He's so young, so tender.

YUDHISHTHIRA: Don't worry. With this driver he could take on the entire earth. *A messenger enters and announces:*

MESSENGER: The troops return! The battle is won!

VIRATA: O happiness! You're sure?

MESSENGER: Yes. Your son is approaching the city, surrounded by cows mooing with joy.

VIRATA: Let his victory be proclaimed at the corner of every street! Send musicians and dancers to greet him! Let all the women offer themselves to him! Bring water for the horses! And for the cows! *Then, addressing Yudhishthira:* Your turn!

YUDHISHTHIRA: It's wrong to play with a happy gambler.

VIRATA: Nonsense. Play.

YUDHISHTHIRA: Gambling is the mother of misfortune. Remember Yudhishthira.

131

VIRATA: I told you to play. It's my day of bliss. *The queen comes in smiling. Virata takes her in his arms and says:* The robbers laid low by my son! What news!

YUDHISHTHIRA: With Vrihannala as his driver, he couldn't be beaten.

VIRATA: My son a conqueror! I roll the word on my tongue.

YUDHISHTHIRA: With this driver, his victory was guaranteed.

VIRATA: What are you saying?

YUDHISHTHIRA: I'm telling you the truth. With this driver he could have conquered the earth.

VIRATA: Have you finished talking about this half-and-half? And insulting my son? Can't you see you're getting on my nerves?

YUDHISHTHIRA: He could even vanquish gods and demons with such a driver.

VIRATA: We'll rip out your tongue. That's enough. Not another word! *He throws a die in Yudhishthira's face, whose nose begins to bleed. Draupadi rushes over and catches the blood.*

GUDESHNA: What are you doing?

DRAUPADI: I'm catching his blood, for it mustn't touch the ground. *At that moment, Uttara and Arjuna enter in triumph.*

VIRATA: My son! Come into my arms! Come and tell me all about your battle! *Uttara notices Yudhishthira:*

UTTARA: Who wounded this man?

VIRATA: I did and he deserved it. I was singing your praises and he could only talk about your driver.

UTTARA: Ask his forgiveness, hurry.

VIRATA: Me, his forgiveness?

YUDHISHTHIRA: You're already forgiven. But if my blood had touched the earth, you would have been in mortal danger—you and your kingdom.

GUDESHNA: Why?

UTTARA: Because this man is Yudhishthira. Because my driver is Arjuna. Because this servant is Draupadi; because here are Bhima, Sahadeva, and Nakula. *The Pandavas reveal themselves to Virata and the others.*

VIRATA: I have to close my eyes. Is it true?

UTTARA: Arjuna fought in my place at the head of your armies. Our enemies hadn't a chance.

VIRATA: You have honored my palace in secret. What can I do for you? Arjuna, take my daughter as your wife.

ARJUNA: No, I'm too old. But I'll take her for my son, Abhimanyu. *He gives some materials to the queen:* Here are the materials you asked for. They're slightly bloodstained, but you can clean them easily.

YUDHISHTHIRA: Virata, we'll soon be leaving, for the period of exile is almost over.

VIRATA: One thought disturbs me, it obsesses me. Answer me before you go: is it true that this world will be destroyed? *Silence. Into the silence comes Vyasa's voice:*

VYASA: It has happened already. *They all listen to Vyasa, who has just come in with the boy.* A long time ago, all living creatures had perished. The world was no more than a sea—a gray, misty, icy swamp. One old man remained, all alone, spared from the devastation. His name was Markandeya. He walked and walked in the stale water, exhausted, finding no shelter anywhere, no trace of life. He was in despair, his throat taut with inexpressible sorrow. Suddenly, not knowing why, he turned and saw behind him a tree rising out of the marsh, a fig tree, and at the foot of the tree a very beautiful, smiling child. *The boy takes up his position.* Markandeya stopped, breathless, reeling, unable to understand why the child was there.

Boy: And the child said to him: "I see you need to rest. Come into my body."

Vyasa: The old man suddenly experienced utter disdain for long life. The child opened his mouth, a great wind rose up, an irresistible gust swept Markandeya toward the mouth. Despite himself he went in, just as he was, and dropped down into the child's belly. There, looking round, he saw a stream, trees, herds of cattle. He saw women carrying water, a city, streets, crowds, rivers. Yes, in the belly of the child he saw the entire earth, calm, beautiful, he saw the ocean, he saw the limitless sky. He walked for a long while, for more than a hundred years, without reaching the end of the body. Then the wind rose up again, he felt himself drawn upward; he came out through the same mouth and saw the child under the fig tree.

Boy: The child looked at him with a smile and said, "I hope you have had a good rest."

# DURYODHANA AND ARJUNA
# WITH KRISHNA

*Krishna is asleep. Duryodhana comes in first and goes to a raised seat at the head of Krishna's bed. Then Arjuna comes in. More modestly, he seats himself at Krishna's feet.*

   *Krishna opens his eyes. He sees Arjuna first, seated directly before him. Then he turns to Duryodhana.*

KRISHNA: Welcome to you both. Why this visit?

DURYODHANA: The earth is throbbing with men on the march. War is drawing near. Krishna, I come to ask you to be our ally.

ARJUNA: I make the same request, in the name of my brothers.

KRISHNA: I've no reason to fight. This is not my war. I was asleep.

DURYODHANA: The whole universe is engaged. No creature can say, "This is not my war." Who can sleep while others die?

KRISHNA: Duryodhana, what is the reason for this war?

DURYODHANA: The Pandavas showed themselves before their time was up. They should go back to the forest for twelve more years. But my father has pardoned them. Let them give up all claim to the kingdom and stay free. *Krishna turns to Arjuna who says to him:*

ARJUNA: My brother Yudhishthira asks for his kingdom. What is his unshakable right, he demands resolutely—now—and he won't wait.

135

DURYODHANA: He will see his elephants with smashed skulls, retching blood. Yudhishthira must be crushed. It's a necessity and it's predicted by every astrologer.

ARJUNA: And I say, I can feel victory walking by my side. My aging eyes see the future clearly. Every night, hungry creatures rise from the underworld and surround me in the hope of a slaughter.

KRISHNA: I love you all. I cannot take sides.

DURYODHANA: It's true. You've shown the same friendship to Arjuna and me. Our family bonds are the same. But I was the first to enter here, I have priority.

KRISHNA: Yes, you were the first to enter. But when I opened my eyes, they fell on Arjuna. It's for him to say what he would prefer. *To Arjuna* On one side I set the mass of my warriors, fully equipped, ready for war. And on the other side, myself, alone, unarmed, taking no part in the battle. Which do you choose?

ARJUNA: I choose you.

KRISHNA: Me, alone, unarmed?

ARJUNA: Yes.

DURYODHANA: That means I have the entire mass of your warriors?

KRISHNA: They are yours.

DURYODHANA: Fully equipped? Determined to fight?

KRISHNA: Determined and faithful.

DURYODHANA: Even to fight against Arjuna?

KRISHNA: Yes, even against him.

DURYODHANA: You yourself won't fight? You won't use your disc?

KRISHNA: I will not fight. *Duryodhana shouts victoriously and leaves.*

KRISHNA: When you chose me, what was in your mind?

ARJUNA: I am strong, I don't need your strength. But I need you to drive my chariot. This thought never leaves me. Be my driver.

KRISHNA: I will drive your chariot. I promise.

# THE EMBASSIES

*A council of war composed of Dhritarashtra and his wife Gandhari, Karna, Duryodhana, and Dushassana. Bhishma and Drona return from a mission.*

DHRITARASHTRA: Bhishma, what did they say? What is the Pandavas' answer to our offer?

BHISHMA: Death is now watching your children. He is already here, observing us, intrigued.

DRONA: They are preparing for war.

BHISHMA: Hundreds of kings accompany them. Each one has chosen his prey.

DHRITARASHTRA: They will come to inform me of the death of my children, of my children's children.

BHISHMA: I don't understand you. Everyone is afraid, everyone suffers!

DURYODHANA: And I am the cause of this suffering. Everyone says so, it's all because of me. But in the past, Bhishma, unaided, conquered all these kings. No one can kill him, we know that. He can't die unless he chooses and we are at his side. Our friends laugh at your fears. They would throw themselves into the fire for us.

DHRITARASHTRA: It's Bhima above all who frightens me. Every night, I wake with this fear. I see his mace above my head.

DURYODHANA: Bhishma, Salva, Jayadratha, Drona, and his son Aswatthaman are there with terrifying weapons. And Karna! We have eleven complete armies against seven. Victory is a fruit in my hand, it's the truth, and I will govern the earth or else I will measure my length in the dust.

DUSHASSANA: Your reign was rich and calm.

DURYODHANA: Yes, so the poets say. All around me I saw happiness. *To Bhishma* Is it true, Bhishma?

BHISHMA: It's true.

DURYODHANA: *To Drona* Is it true, Drona?

DRONA: It's true.

DURYODHANA: Nobody is calling for our enemies to return. I was given a kingdom which I stamped with a number: One. I won't mutilate this kingdom, I won't skin it alive. I will leave it intact as it was given. I will never share it, I yield nothing.

DHRITARASHTRA: *To Bhishma* And Krishna? You've seen him?

BHISHMA: He is with them.

DURYODHANA: You're afraid of Krishna?

GANDHARI: It's him above all that I fear.

DURYODHANA: He has given me his powerful armies. Is that a way to destroy me?

DUSHASSANA: No one knows what Krishna intends.

DURYODHANA: People say he's close to the gods. I am too. My powers are divine, they are irresistible, magical. Yes, I can sing the wind and the rain into submission, I can harden water. No demon, no sorcerer can harm me. No storm nor fire can protect those I hate!

KARNA: If the gods were on Yudhishthira's side, he would never have lost at dice.

DURYODHANA: I never lost.

KARNA: I will kill Arjuna. I learned this in a dream and my dreams are true.

BHISHMA: Karna, this earth that you despise and walk on with such pride will strike you one day. It will drag you down and you will cry to heaven in vain.

KARNA: *To Bhishma* You always treat me like an imbecile and a coward. Is it because of your great age?

BHISHMA: Old I may be, as you enjoy repeating, still I don't know a warrior anywhere who is my equal.

KARNA: Not even Arjuna? Not even me?

BHISHMA: No one.

KARNA: Not even Drona?

BHISHMA: Not even Drona. *Drona nods in agreement.*

DURYODHANA: *To Bhishma* In that case, I ask and you can't refuse: take command. Be our general.

BHISHMA: Me?

KARNA: Aren't you the best? The invincible? The incomparable? The one who is impossible to kill?

BHISHMA: Duryodhana, I've always lived without a kingdom. Don't impose this burden on me.

KARNA: Everything that's threatening us, everything that's tearing us apart comes from you, from the lunatic promise you made long ago, long before we were born—never a woman, never a child. Your interminable, useless life you have spent here, eating and drinking from the king's hand. If you shrink from the battle, your white life will be stained. You can't refuse. I wouldn't hesitate. What I owe, I pay.

DHRITARASHTRA: Bhishma, accept the commandment. With you and Drona, there'd be no more risk and I'd never again be afraid. Who knows, perhaps they'll give up the thought of war.

DURYODHANA: You accept?

KARNA: Or you're afraid of death, after all?

BHISHMA: I'm afraid of everything except death. Yes, I accept, but on one condition: Karna must not fight.

DURYODHANA: Why?

BHISHMA: I can't say why.

DURYODHANA: Are you afraid his light might outshine yours?

BHISHMA: No. That's not what I fear.

DURYODHANA: Then why leave Karna idle? *Bhishma does not answer. He stays silent. In the silence, Karna seizes his sword and throws it at Bhishma's feet saying:*

KARNA: Here. I will only fight after your death. *He leaves, followed by Duryodhana and Drona. Bhishma is alone with the royal couple, Dhritarashtra and Gandhari. He picks up Karna's sword and looks at it. Night is falling. Dhritarashtra asks:*

DHRITARASHTRA: Bhishma, are you there?

BHISHMA: Yes.

DHRITARASHTRA: Is it night?

BHISHMA: Yes, it's already dark.

DHRITARASHTRA: I'm reassured. I thank you. They say the blind are not made to lead the world, but those who see tear one another apart and kill. *Bhishma says nothing. He is still looking at Karna's sword.* Gandhari?

GANDHARI: I am here.

DHRITARASHTRA: I dread the moment of sleep. Something keeps me awake, every night. Sometimes I open my eyes and sense the presence of evil.

GANDHARI: Hate burns your sons and the same hate clouds your reason. You want to keep what isn't yours.

BHISHMA: A single one of your thoughts could destroy the world. You haven't the right to be foolish.

GANDHARI: Give your nephews back their kingdom.

DHRITARASHTRA: A deathless boy, very young and very old, once said to me: "Death doesn't exist." What did he mean?

BHISHMA: Ask him. He is here. *An ageless ascetic has appeared in the dimly lit room.*

DHRITARASHTRA: Are you the deathless boy?

ASCETIC: Yes.

DHRITARASHTRA: You said "Death does not exist"?

ASCETIC: I did.

DHRITARASHTRA: Yet even gods make sacrifices so as not to die.

ASCETIC: Both things are true. Poets pay homage to death, they glorify it in song. But I tell you death is negligence. It is ignorance, and vigilance is immortality. Death is a tiger crouching in the brush; we create children for death. But death cannot devour a man who has shaken off his dust; it is powerless against eternity. The wind, life, flow from the infinite, the moon drinks the breath of life, the sun drinks the moon, and the infinite drinks the sun. The wise man soars between the worlds. When his body is destroyed, when no trace of it remains, then death itself is destroyed and he contemplates infinity. I said farewell to myself and I see myself in all beings. I am all that is not yet here, all that is still to come. I am the ancestor. I am space. The cause of my birth is myself. I am the limit of everything; tireless, indestructible. *The ascetic sits down a little to one side.*

BHISHMA: Above this world and below this world there is nothing but darkness, and so it is in the mystery of your heart.

DHRITARASHTRA: Stay close to me all night. *A moment's silence. Then Duryodhana and Dushassana enter.*

DURYODHANA: Krishna is on his way.

DHRITARASHTRA: Krishna?

DURYODHANA: He comes in embassy, sent by Yudhishthira. *Dushassana says to his brother:*

DUSHASSANA: This is the perfect moment. Let's seize Krishna and put him in irons.

DURYODHANA: *To Dushassana* Yes. I like your idea. I already have all his armies. I'll keep him prisoner.

GANDHARI: No! Krishna brings danger, don't touch him!

DHRITARASHTRA: Quick! Prepare him a palace. And perfumes, precious stones! Let the whole city gaze upon him! Send him young naked girls! Sprinkle water before him!

KRISHNA: It's not worth the trouble. I'm here. *They turn toward Krishna, who has just come in.*

DHRITARASHTRA: The seat of honor, quick! Refreshments, fans! *Krishna waves away the seat of honor that is presented to him and sits on the ground. He stops the music. Drona offers him refreshments which he refuses too.*

DRONA: Why do you refuse?

KRISHNA: Ambassadors only receive honors at the end of their mission. These refreshments must be eaten in joy.

DHRITARASHTRA: Yudhishthira has sent you?

KRISHNA: Yes.

DHRITARASHTRA: We don't understand why.

DURYODHANA: What is your purpose?

KRISHNA: *To Dhritarashtra* Dhritarashtra, my words are for you. You haven't forgotten that the Pandavas, your five nephews, were raised by you, they are like your sons. You must give them what is theirs. There is nothing more to say.

DHRITARASHTRA: Krishna, I'm not the master. I can't answer for myself. Speak to my son.

KRISHNA: *To Duryodhana* You wish to listen?

DURYODHANA: I'm listening.

KRISHNA: You're of noble blood, you are learned, your qualities are real. You raise your voice and you're obeyed. But you are destroying your life. The man who scorns advice burns his stomach as though with green fruit. His friends groan for a moment, then disaster catches him up. The earth loathes and rejects him. You long for omnipotence, for total splendor, but stay master of yourself and don't despise others.

DHRITARASHTRA: *To Duryodhana* Bow down before Yudhishthira, lay your pride at his feet. He will raise you up, he will put his hand on your shoulder. Bhima will clasp you in his arms.

BHISHMA: Don't oblige me to kill my family.

DRONA: Don't compel me to fight Arjuna.

DHRITARASHTRA: Enjoy the earth like brothers.

DURYODHANA: *To Krishna* When you speak, it's always me you blame. And the others as well, everything falls on me, always me. You all hate me and yet I've never committed the least fault, never! It was Sakuni who won; it wasn't my doing. I have one question to put to you, Krishna: do you believe in the possibility of peace?

KRISHNA: I think what I say is possible, otherwise I would not say it.

DURYODHANA: But in the depths of your heart, if you listen without lying, don't you hear the growl of war?

KRISHNA: Can a war without a winner be a war? Could a man with his eyes open plunge into war knowing that everyone will die?

DURYODHANA: Everyone keeps telling me I can't win. Very well, death by arms is a grand death, the best of deaths. I will never bow down.

KRISHNA: As I was leaving, Yudhishthira called me back and said, "I have chosen five villages: Avisthala, Vrikartala, Makandi, Varanavata, and Avasaba. Let Dhritarashtra leave us these five villages and there'll be no war."

DURYODHANA: A king does not stake his kingdom. A king does not stoop to ask for five villages. I will not give five villages. I will not give one village. I will not give the point of a needle of earth.

*Krishna speaks very forcefully:*

KRISHNA: Let one thing be certain: you will have your grand death! If the earth is clamoring for victims, we will see a splendid massacre. The game of dice was a fraud, as well you know! Draupadi was dragged in public and you say: "I haven't committed a single fault"? *Duryodhana and Dushassana storm out, furious. To the king* Quick, call them back. They want to take hold of me!

BHISHMA: Like madmen, like children.

KRISHNA: Your son wants to make me his hostage, so much the worse for him.

DHRITARASHTRA: *To Krishna* Wait! Don't go!

GANDHARI: Krishna, spare him! *Duryodhana has reappeared with Dushassana. They are armed and threatening. Gandhari tries to calm Duryodhana:* My son, your hatred's for yourself. After thirteen years of anger, try to be calm.

KRISHNA: Duryodhana, you think I'm alone?

DRONA: You want to take hold of Krishna? You don't know who he is?

BHISHMA: You think he's defenseless? Look—look carefully. *Everyone looks at Krishna, who is smiling. Vyasa and the boy hold a thin curtain in front of him. Music rises.* When he laughs, thirteen tongues of fire spring from his mouth. Brahma sits on his bow; the guardians of the world stand on his arms. I see the Adityas, the Sadhyas, the Vasus; above him vast armies are assembled. From his eyes, his nose, his ears billow fire and smoke—heavenly, universal, terrible form. Rays of light stream from his skin. . . . *Most are prostrate, except Duryodhana and Dushassana.*

DHRITARASHTRA: Lighten my eyes for a moment, I beg you, let me see you!

KRISHNA: Yes, here are eyes. *Krishna gestures toward Dhritarashtra.*

DHRITARASHTRA: I see you. *A moment's silence. All are watching in wonder.*

BHISHMA: Out of chaos, a miracle . . .

DHRITARASHTRA: My son, can you see as I do?

BHISHMA: *To Duryodhana* Can you see? *Duryodhana does not reply and leaves abruptly with Dushassana.*

DHRITARASHTRA: Where are you going? Come back. Listen to us! Look!

BHISHMA: The flames slowly die down, the universe vanishes, the light fades. He resumes the form of a man.

DHRITARASHTRA: Darkness covers me again. I can no longer distinguish anything. Krishna, Krishna, I did what I could.

KRISHNA: So did I. *Krishna rises. Dhritarashtra and Gandhari leave together.*

# KRISHNA'S LAST EFFORTS

*Krishna stays alone with Bhishma who is deep in thought.*

KRISHNA: Where are your thoughts, Bhishma?

BHISHMA: Fixed on what I must do.

KRISHNA: You have agreed to take command. You will fight.

BHISHMA: Yes.

KRISHNA: Withdraw. Nothing ties you to this war.

BHISHMA: I cannot betray those who have fed me.

KRISHNA: Close your eyes. Descend into the secret recesses of your heart. Are you sure, despite your love of peace, that you are not following an obscure desire to show your supremacy?

BHISHMA: My place is here. You know it. *With these words, he leaves. Kunti appears and asks Krishna:*

KUNTI: Krishna, are you leaving?

KRISHNA: Yes, Kunti. What shall I say to your sons, whom you haven't seen for so many years? That I found you sad and silent? That you burn with desire to see them again?

KUNTI: No, don't say that. Tell Yudhishthira that a bad king is a contagious disease, that he perverts his age. Tell him he was not born for a meager life. Say to him awake, arise, or else you are just a hole infested with rats, a contented worm.

KRISHNA: Your son could answer me. What could a piece of land mean to me, or pleasure, or life?

KUNTI: Answer him, he is not alone. For all the creatures around him, he is the center. If he is lacking in resolution, his great opponent, misery, will grow rich from his weakness. Tell him I was once a young and beautiful sovereign laden with garlands. He never knew me, but he will know me starving. He will see me broken and demented.

KRISHNA: And if he says to you you have shut your heart to pity?

KUNTI: Kindness has no power and its taste is bitter. Forge yourself a heart of iron, for pity is a poison.

KRISHNA: And my body? I feel tenderly toward my body.

KUNTI: I would tell my son: your body is beautiful, your body is noble, but if you live with the fear of death, why were you given life? Burn like a torch, if only for an instant, rather than smolder for a long while. Tell him this besides: be the enemy of your enemies; send spies to watch over them. Be strong and the strong will come to you, or else my words have lost their light. Speak to Arjuna, speak to Madri's children, whom I regard as my own, speak to Draupadi—she understands me—speak to Bhima, tell him it is for this moment that a woman bears a son. If he lets it pass, he will be sterile and I will reject him for ever.

KRISHNA: And Karna? *Kunti remains silent for an instant. She lowers her voice to answer:*

KUNTI: He has thrown down his sword. I know it, he will not fight.

KRISHNA: And if Bhishma eventually meets his death? If Karna joins the battle? *Kunti says nothing.* I am going back to your sons. Have you anything else to say to them?

KUNTI: Tell them I am keeping well. *Kunti leaves. Karna's voice is heard, saying:*

KARNA: That was Kunti?

KRISHNA: Yes, that was Kunti. You were looking for me?

KARNA: No, I was walking by myself in the palace. Sometimes I like to be alone. I go my own way, you know, closed, confused, plagued by rumors. Him whom I call father and her whom I call mother are not my father and mother.

KRISHNA: Karna, you are the son of Kunti. *Karna receives this revelation, but says nothing.* You were born before her marriage, but when a woman already has a child, he becomes the child of the man she marries. You know that. *Karna nods his head.* You are therefore Pandu's son. That's why Bhishma wished to prevent you from fighting. Because your enemies are your brothers.

KARNA: They know it?

KRISHNA: No, but if I reveal your birth to them, they will bring you perfumes and gold, and on the sixth day Draupadi will be your wife. Bhima will carry your fan, Arjuna will drive your chariot, I myself will follow you. Your brothers, your friends, your mother will be happy. Duryodhana will no longer dare to fight.

KARNA: My mother abandoned me, abandoned me to chance, to a river's whim. A chariot driver found me and took me home. His wife washed away my urine and my excrement, the driver gave me his warmth. Neither the earth itself nor mountains of gold, neither joy nor fear could make me change my feelings. I have given my word. I won't take it back. Don't reveal my birth. As I was born before him, Yudhishthira would want to give me his crown and I would pass it on to Duryodhana, because I am the son of a driver. May Yudhishthira have a long reign. Everything I've said to wound him I regret. Krishna, we are going to celebrate the great sacrifice of arms and the eye that lights on everything will be yours. We will have drums and cries of war; we will have blood, and skulls in which to drink the blood. The sacrifice will invade the night. When you see me stretched out dead, when you see Bhima devour Dushassana's guts, when Bhishma and Drona are destroyed, when you hear the women wail, the sacrifice will be over. Dispose of everything. I know what you want.

KRISHNA: I give you the earth and you reject it.

KARNA: Put Arjuna in front of me and do not tell him I'm his mother's son.

KRISHNA: The victory of the Pandavas is assured. Tell your friends, "Look, it's spring, the buds are sweet, the water sparkles, everyone is joyful. We are going to die."

KARNA: You who know me so well, why do you trouble me? If you are here to bring the earth to its end, very well, the time has come.

KRISHNA: No, I'm not here to destroy.

KARNA: Flesh and blood rain from the sky. Bodiless voices cry in the night. Horses weep. One-eyed, one-legged monstrosities hop across the land. Birds perch on flags with fire in their beaks crying "Ripe! It's ripe!" A cow gives birth to an ass, a woman to a jackal. Newborn babies dance. Sons learn to be men between their mothers' thighs. Statues write with their weapons. Torches no longer give light. Cripples laugh. The different races merge. Vultures come to prayer. The setting sun is surrounded by disfigured corpses. Time will destroy the universe. I'm racked all night by my dreams. I dreamed of you, surrounded by bleeding entrails. I dreamed of Yudhishthira, radiant, mounted on a pile of bones, drinking from a golden goblet. I know from where victory will come.

KRISHNA: You must be right. If I can't touch your heart, the ruin of the earth is near.

KARNA: One thing is certain, Krishna. We will make a great journey together.

KRISHNA: Yes, and we will find each other again, one day. *They embrace.*

PART III

THE WAR

# THE BHAGAVAD-GITA

*All the armies are assembled for battle. The kings and their warriors are facing one another. There is a roll of drums. Yudhishthira goes toward Dhritarashtra, saying:*

YUDHISHTHIRA: Dhritarashtra, you have chosen war. It is here. Now, all is ready—my warriors, my horses, my chariots, my elephants, many millions of weapons, convoys, food stores, forges, tents for the wounded, logs for the funeral pyres, musicians, soothsayers, prostitutes, poisonous snakes. My orders are given, my armies shake the earth. Listen, Bhima is blowing his conch, you recognize his breath? Arjuna, with Krishna at his reins, will give the signal and the battle you wish for will begin.

DHRITARASHTRA: We must fix the rules of war.

YUDHISHTHIRA: Speak!

DHRITARASHTRA: Never fight at night. Never strike a man who has withdrawn from the fray, nor a man fighting with words.

YUDHISHTHIRA: And never strike in the back, nor on the legs.

DHRITARASHTRA: Is Vyasa here?

VYASA: Yes, I am always here.

DHRITARASHTRA: You who are composing this poem, do you know who will win?

VYASA: The future does not exist, Dhritarashtra. But I can give you eyes to see the battle.

DHRITARASHTRA: No, I don't want to see my children die. Sanjaya will tell me everything.

VYASA: Sanjaya, you will be the king's eye. I will give you a special power: without moving you will see every detail of the battlefield.

SANJAYA: Yes, I see the north and the south, the east and the west. I see many millions of men, as far as the horizon, and I see the look on every face.

DHRITARASHTRA: Stay by my side.
    *Dhritarashtra and Gandhari stay with Sanjaya. Opposite them, Kunti is sitting with Draupadi. Vyasa moves away. Gandhari calls him back:*

GANDHARI: Vyasa, are you leaving?

VYASA: Yes, I'm going to prepare for the dead.

GANDHARI: Who is going to die? Who will be your victims?

KUNTI: Vyasa, you find too much beauty in men's death. Blood decorates your poem, and the cries of the dying are your music.

VYASA: Don't throw this growing horror onto me. Each of you could have made this war impossible.

BOY: I don't want to see people die. Can I stay with the king? *Vyasa nods and leaves.*
    *In the Pandava camp, Arjuna is alone, in prayer. Draupadi comes up to him.*

DRAUPADI: Arjuna, the two armies are face to face, their great lines, glittering with pride, seem without end. All the peoples of the world are there, hungry for the earth, ready to hurl themselves on one another like dogs on a scrap of flesh. For fourteen years I've been waiting for this moment. *Arjuna says nothing. He looks at her.*

DRAUPADI: Krishna has prepared your chariot. He is checking your weapons. He is speaking to your horses. Everything is in your hands. You know it. *Arjuna nods gently.*

DRAUPADI: What god have you chosen to protect you today?

ARJUNA: I've chosen the black goddess, she who wears a chain of deaths round her neck. I have chosen Kali.

DRAUPADI: And if one of these deaths should be yours? Arjuna, when I think of you, my skin goes dry and I shake. My confidence goes. *They embrace. As they do so, Krishna appears. Krishna and Arjuna leave together. Draupadi goes out on the other side. All the warriors except Arjuna now appear, ready for the confrontation. At this moment, Yudhishthira leaves the Pandavas' ranks, lays down his arms, and walks alone toward the Kauravas. Bhima follows, trying to hold him back.*

BHIMA: Yudhishthira, where are you going, alone and unarmed? Are you afraid at the last moment? What do you want with our enemies? *Yudhishthira comes to where Bhishma stands and says:*

YUDHISHTHIRA: Bhishma, I touch your feet. We are going to fight against you, you whom no one can kill. Grant me leave to strike you.

BHISHMA: If you hadn't come to me, Yudhishthira, I would have hated and despised you. I am chained to your enemies. Commit yourself to the struggle and fight until you win. *Yudhishthira crosses to Drona:*

YUDHISHTHIRA: Drona, I touch your feet. We will fight against you; you who made us. Grant me leave to strike you.

DRONA: If you hadn't come to me, I too would have despised you. I too am chained to your enemies. I too wish for your victory.

YUDHISHTHIRA: Fight with them, but think of me.

DRONA: You cannot be beaten.

YUDHISHTHIRA: You promise us victory?

DRONA: So long as Bhishma and I are alive, that victory is impossible.

YUDHISHTHIRA: Victory and defeat are impossible?

DRONA: That's what I say.

YUDHISHTHIRA: Is there a way of killing you?

DRONA: No, not unless I lay down my arms to prepare for death.

YUDHISHTHIRA: Before whom could you lay down your arms? *Drona is silent for a moment, then he answers:*

DRONA: Before a man of truth, the day he chooses to lie. *Yudhishthira returns to his camp, saying to himself:*

YUDHISHTHIRA: Now, the battle begins. *The warriors take their positions for the battle.*

GANDHARI: I hear a chariot.

SANJAYA: Arjuna, led by Krishna, is advancing between the two armies. They stop. Arjuna grasps his conch to launch the battle. He looks one way then the other, he sees Bhishma, he sees Drona, he sees his cousins, his friends.

ARJUNA: Krishna, my legs grow weak, my mouth is dry, my body trembles, my bow slips from my hands, my skin burns, I can no longer stand. What good can come from this battle? My family will be massacred. If this is the price, who can wish for victory, or pleasure, or even life? Uncles, cousins, nephews, and Drona, my teacher— they are all there. I can't bring death to my own family. What happiness could that give? All pleasure would be stained in blood. No, I prefer not to defend myself. I will wait here for death.

DHRITARASHTRA: What's he doing?

SANJAYA: He has thrown down his bow and his arrows.

GANDHARI: He has thrown down his bow and his arrows.

DURYODHANA: Arjuna has thrown down his bow and his arrows?

DUSHASSANA: Arjuna refuses to fight?

YUDHISHTHIRA: Why does he bow his head? Where is his pride? Where is his wish to fight?

KRISHNA: What is this mad and shameful weakness? Stand up.

ARJUNA: How can I aim my arrows at Bhishma, at Drona? I am in anguish, my resolution's gone. I'm shaking, I can't see where my duty lies. Teach me.

KRISHNA: Victory and defeat, pleasure and pain are all the same. Act, but don't reflect on the fruits of the act. Forget desire; seek detachment.

ARJUNA: Yet you urge me to battle, to massacre. Your words are ambiguous. I am confused.

KRISHNA: Renunciation is not enough. You must not withdraw into solitude. You must not stay without action, for we are here to serve the world.

ARJUNA: Yes, I know.

KRISHNA: You must rise up free from hope and throw yourself into the battle.

ARJUNA: I cannot. *Krishna murmurs in his ear.* How can I put into practice what you're demanding of me? The mind is capricious, unstable; it's evasive, feverish, turbulent, tenacious. It's harder to subdue than taming the wind.

KRISHNA: It's true.
    You must learn to see with the same eye a mound of earth and a heap of gold, a cow and a sage, a dog and the man who eats the dog. The mind is greater than the senses. Above the mind there is pure

intelligence, freed from thought. Beyond pure intelligence there is being—universal being. That is where you live, where we all live.

ARJUNA: All the time, we are swept away. How can I decide? How can I choose? With what will? We are dragged toward evil, as though compelled. Why?

KRISHNA: There is a way to rid oneself of this poison.

ARJUNA: What is this way?

KRISHNA: *changing his tone* To reply to his question, Krishna led Arjuna through the tangled forest of illusion. He began to teach him the ancient yoga of wisdom and the mysterious path of action. He spoke for a long time, a very long time, between the two armies preparing to destroy themselves.

ARJUNA: All men are born into illusion. How can one reach the truth if one is born in illusion?

KRISHNA: Slowly Krishna led Arjuna through all the fibers of his spirit. He showed him the deepest movements of his being and his true battlefield where you need neither warriors nor arrows, where each man must fight alone. It's the most secret knowledge. He showed him the whole of truth; he taught him how the world unfolds.

ARJUNA: I feel my illusions vanish, one by one. Now, if I'm capable of contemplating it, show me your universal form.

I can't count your mouths, nor your eyes, nor your jewels, your clothes, your weapons. Astonishing vision, all-penetrating form, magnificent, endless, as though a thousand suns rise in the sky. I see you, in one point I see the entire world. All the warriors hurl themselves into your mouth and you grind them between your teeth. They wish to be destroyed and you destroy them. Through your body I see the stars, I see life and death, I see silence. Tell me who are you. I am shaken to the depths and I'm afraid.

KRISHNA: Matter changes but I am all that you say, all that you think. Everything rests on me like pearls on a thread. I am the earth's scent and the fire's heat. I am appearance and disappearance. I am the trickster's hoax. I am the radiance of all that shines. All beings fall in the night and all beings are brought back to daylight. I have already defeated all these warriors, but he who thinks he can kill and he who thinks he can be killed are both mistaken. No weapon can pierce the life that informs you; no fire can burn it; no water can drench it; no wind can make it dry. Have no fear and rise up, because I love you. *After a short silence, Krishna continues:* Then Krishna resumed his kind and benevolent form. He said to Arjuna: "Now you can dominate your mysterious, incomprehensible spirit, you can see its other side. Act as you must act. I myself am never without action. Rise up."

ARJUNA: My illusion is dissolved, my error destroyed. Thanks to you my understanding has returned. Now I am firm. My doubts are dispersed, I will act according to your word. *Suddenly Duryodhana cries out:*

DURYODHANA: When will they stop talking? If Arjuna refuses to fight, if he's paralyzed with fear, let him go back to the woods with his brothers and let me reign. *Arjuna blows on his conch, giving the signal for battle. The battle begins. Bhishma leads the Kauravas, who seem to be winning.*

GANDHARI: Already, torn flesh, stomachs ripped, stamping elephants crushing chests; fathers can't recognize their sons. The dying cry: "It's me! Do I know you? Don't move! Don't leave me!" Enemy hooked to enemy, bolted together with iron.

DHRITARASHTRA: Sanjaya, can you see Bhishma?

SANJAYA: Yes, he bestrides the battle. He plays it like a dance. He's fire without smoke, irresistible energy. He cuts off hundreds of heads without emotion.

DHRITARASHTRA: These cries, what do they say?

GANDHARI: It's Bhima shouting at Dushassana: "I'll kill you, I'll kill you!"

DHRITARASHTRA: He will kill him. Nothing can save my son.

GANDHARI: You permitted the game of dice. What you sowed, you reap.

*The Pandavas launch a counterattack. Night falls and a bugle halts the battle. The fighters retire.*

  *Bhishma is being massaged in his tent. Drona, Duryodhana, Dushassana, and Karna (who has not been fighting) enter. Duryodhana says to Bhishma:*

DURYODHANA: Bhishma, you launched these attacks and you have been thrown back. By what sorcery? You, whose strength is legendary. You, the only stranger to death—are you on our enemies' side?

BHISHMA: I have Arjuna and Bhima against me. I've already told you—my voice is hoarse from telling you—Krishna's their guide.
*Karna says to Duryodhana, without directly addressing Bhishma:*

KARNA: Bhishma loves battles—the cries, the frenzy, the warm smell of death. Blood feeds his pride. Yet he pities those he fights. Let him withdraw and I will take his place.

DURYODHANA: Yes, if you have fear or pity, withdraw.

BHISHMA: Why do you lacerate me when I'm killing my family for you? Your thoughts are like ashes, your mind gropes in the dark. The man who is about to die sees all the trees covered with gold. You are going to die.

DUSHASSANA: I saw Bhima hurl himself toward me, crying: "I'll kill you! I'll kill you!"

DURYODHANA: Bhishma, you have failed me. Now, instantly, I demand victory.

BHISHMA: Tomorrow. Tomorrow will be my greatest battle. Leave me alone. *Duryodhana, Karna, and Dushassana leave. As Drona is about to go, Bhishma calls to him:* Drona. *Drona stops. His son Aswatthaman remains behind him.* Ask your son to leave.

DRONA: Aswatthaman . . . *Aswatthaman withdraws.*

BHISHMA: You love your son?

DRONA: He's all I have.

BHISHMA: I saw a stranger in a dream. He cried out: "I bear Drona's death."

DRONA: Did he say why he wanted to kill me?

BHISHMA: He said you know. *Drona thinks for a moment, then says:*

DRONA: No one knows why he has to die, except you. *He goes. Bhishma is alone, pensive.*

BHISHMA: Yes, that's true. *Then he becomes aware of a woman who has just appeared. It is Amba. Her clothes are tattered, she is very pale. Bhishma is the only one to see her.*

BHISHMA: Is it you, Amba?

AMBA: As you see.

BHISHMA: I wait for you every night.

AMBA: I know.

BHISHMA: Give up this madness. Stop hunting me across the earth; accept being at peace at last.

AMBA: I bring you strange news. I am dead. *Bhishma remains silent. She continues:* No one wished to fight against you. Alone, I climbed to the snows that cover the roof of the world, seeking to know how death can outwit death. In the icy fog and the biting wind, for twelve years, I stayed upright and rigid on one toe, waiting for the voice of a god. I turned into rock, I became snow. After twelve years, a voice rang out, commanding: "Gather bark, twigs, moss." I did so. "Make a pile of dry wood." I did so. "Rub flints together, light the wood, wait until the flames hide the sky." My eyes open, I threw myself onto the fire. My skin crackled, the smell reached my nostrils, I choked. I was in pain, I cried out, I am dead.

BHISHMA: You are dead?

AMBA: Yes.

BHISHMA: So you've lost your desire to kill me?

AMBA: No. *Bhishma says nothing. Amba resumes.* In death's gray zone, I waited for my new strength. I was neither above nor below, neither in nor out—sweating, ice-cold, with one single image before my eyes: yours Bhishma. I had burnt myself for you and now I knew another birth. Here is my second surprise. I'm taking part in this battle and I'm now a man.

BHISHMA: What is your name?

AMBA: I've a man's shape, a man's sex. One thing is sure, it never wavers: in the depths of my heart—a woman's heart—there's only you, Bhishma, you alone for all time. My name is now Sikhandin. Sikhandin. *She goes.*

  *Then Arjuna, Krishna, and Yudhishthira enter, coming to visit Bhishma in his own camp under cover of night. He gestures to them to sit.*

ARJUNA: After nine days of battle, victory eludes us. Our banners are tattered, our chariots smashed, our finest horsemen beheaded. Death and blood spurt from your hand and we are drowning in them. Bhishma, how can we defeat you? You must tell us.

BHISHMA: As long as I'm alive, that is impossible. You must kill me first. If I die, everything dies.

YUDHISHTHIRA: But you can choose when to die. How can we kill you?

BHISHMA: No one can kill me, so long as I carry my arms.

KRISHNA: And if you laid down your arms?

BHISHMA: Yes, if I laid down my arms and I accepted to die, yes, then you could kill me.

ARJUNA: Who could make you lay down your arms?

BHISHMA: An unarmed man, a cripple, the father of an only son, a woman. *He addresses Yudhishthira:* You want me to die, Yudhishthira? You are asking me to die?

YUDHISHTHIRA: You brought us up. How could I want you to die?

ARJUNA: Yet you must understand, as no one can kill you, the massacre will continue until no life remains.

YUDHISHTHIRA: I've made my decision. I must stop the war. *A moment's pause.*

BHISHMA: No. There's a man fighting in your ranks, the only man capable of killing me.

KRISHNA: Who?

BHISHMA: Sikhandin. Yes, if I saw Sikhandin before me, I could not fight and he could kill me.

KRISHNA: Why?

BHISHMA: No. I'll say no more. Kill me if you wish, but grant me the secret of my death. Arjuna, put Sikhandin in the lead tomorrow, tell him to raise his bow and strike.

ARJUNA: When I was a child, you used to take me on your knee. I'd soil your clothes with my dusty feet. I called you father. How can I tell someone to strike you?

BHISHMA: It's lawful to kill an old man, however virtuous, when he comes toward you bearing your death. *Bhishma straightens. Arjuna, Krishna, and Yudhishthira leave. Dawn is breaking, Bhishma returns to battle. Dhritarashtra asks Sanjaya:*

DHRITARASHTRA: Has the sun risen?

SANJAYA: Yes, it's misty and red.

DHRITARASHTRA: Is Bhishma back in the field?

SANJAYA: Yes, he's the first to advance. He strikes without seeming to move, his hands launch columns of air and the shattered armies retreat. *Amba, who has become the warrior Sikhandin, appears.*

BOY: A man is coming toward him, alone.

DHRITARASHTRA: Alone?

GANDHARI: A young warrior. He walks. He stops.

BOY: He hesitates. He goes back again.

DHRITARASHTRA: Who is this young madman? What does he want? Hasn't Bhishma already killed him?

SANJAYA: No. Bhishma has just seen him. He doesn't move.

BOY: He lowers his arms.

DHRITARASHTRA: Bhishma? Why? Has his chariot been broken? Has his bow been snapped?

SANJAYA: They are facing one another. *Amba is now a man. She is Sikhandin. She carries arms and wears men's clothes. Arjuna is behind her/him. Krishna is not far from them. The young warrior asks Bhishma:*

AMBA–SIKHANDIN: Do you recognize me?

BHISHMA: You are Sikhandin.

AMBA–SIKHANDIN: Yes, that's my name. Your long life has reached its end. Take a last look at this world you'll see no more.

BHISHMA: I've still got my weapons. I can't leave without one last fight. Attack me. *Bhishma challenges Sikhandin who lifts his bow.*

ARJUNA: Go close to him. Only you can kill him. *Suddenly Amba–Sikhandin hesitates.*

AMBA–SIKHANDIN: At the very last moment, my hand shakes. How can I kill this immense old man? My mind is darkening.

ARJUNA: His spirit has already left him. He's just a twitching bag of flesh. Attack him!

AMBA–SIKHANDIN: Who was I before I became a man?

ARJUNA: Go close to him! Look him in the face! Attack!

AMBA–SIKHANDIN: I can't raise my arm. *Arjuna pushes Sikhandin, who now faces Bhishma. Bhishma drops his fighting pose.*

BHISHMA: Amba, in memory of a long-past day, I now bring the slaughter to its end. Arjuna and Yudishthira, listen to me. My body drops away. It's wounded and dismayed. The day and the moment have come.

ARJUNA: *To Sikhandin* Shoot your arrow! You threw yourself into the fire to kill him.

AMBA–SIKHANDIN: Why does he call me Amba? Why such hate? Where was it born? I can't remember. *Krishna says to Arjuna:*

KRISHNA: You, quick, shoot an arrow! Don't let him take back his life!

ARJUNA: I can't.

KRISHNA: Shoot an arrow. *Sheltered by Sikhandin, Arjuna shoots an arrow at Bhishma. The arrow moves through the air with infinite slowness and hits the old man. He staggers.*

BHISHMA: The precise arrow that kills me, Sikhandin, is not yours. You didn't shoot it. It enters my flesh like a snake. It's Arjuna's arrow. *The warriors prepare a bed of arrows. Bhishma is laid on it.*

DHRITARASHTRA: Has Bhishma fallen?

SANJAYA: He's not dead. His chest still rises and falls. A thousand arrows pierce him.

DHRITARASHTRA: Bring me to him. Stop the battle. *Krishna goes up to Arjuna, who is looking dejected, and says to him:*

KRISHNA: You didn't kill him. He decided to end his life.

ARJUNA: I loved him.

KRISHNA: You are my best friend, yet no doubt you'll see me die. *Sanjaya leads Dhritarashtra and Gandhari to Bhishma, who is surrounded by the warriors.*

DHRITARASHTRA: Can you hear my voice? *Bhishma replies in a feeble voice:*

BHISHMA: Yes, I hear the blind man's voice. My head is falling backwards. Arjuna, give me the pillow I need. *Arjuna shoots two arrows. Bhishma leans his head on them.*

DHRITARASHTRA: Bhishma, without you my confidence goes. I've known you all my life, you've been my guide. Can you really die?

BHISHMA: I will stay on this bed until the sun reaches its zenith. At that moment I will die. I will reach the eternal region. I'm already on the other bank and it's from there that I speak.

*Karna has just appeared. He goes to the bed of arrows.*

BHISHMA: I hear Karna's steps.

KARNA: I've always been an object of hate for you.

BHISHMA: Give me your hand. *Karna hesitates then places his hand in Bhishma's.* You betray your nature. You detest those who have the qualities you lack. But you are strong and profound, as strong as Arjuna. I ask you, Karna, unite, paralyze the war, live peacefully on this earth.

KARNA: Duryodhana gave me everything, I will keep faith with him.

BHISHMA: One is only faithful to death. I too kept faith. I too am dead.

KARNA: They say the Pandavas can't be defeated. I say I will defeat them. Grant me your permission to fight.

BHISHMA: If you wished, you could be like an ocean to the rivers, you could be the cloud that brings rain.

KARNA: I beg you, speak to me favorably before you enter the world of the dead.

BHISHMA: Can you fight without anger, without pride?

KARNA: Yes. Give me your leave.

BHISHMA: Go then, join the battle, since life seems to you so trifling, and set me facing the east, toward the rising sun. *Karna stands motionless, erect, while Bhishma is carried away.*

KARNA: Prepare my weapons, bring out my chariot, raise my flag! *Duryodhana takes Karna in his arms.*

DURYODHANA: My army has found its protector.

KARNA: Give me your orders.

DURYODHANA: For ten days Bhishma has been our chief. Who can follow him? Choose. *Karna's eye falls on Drona who is still prostrate on the ground.*

KARNA: You must name Drona, the finest of us all.

DURYODHANA: Aswatthaman, raise your father. *Aswatthaman helps his father to his feet.* Drona, take command. I request victory of you.

DRONA: *To Karna* Why not you, Karna?

KARNA: Because I could not give you orders.

DRONA: You will accept mine?

KARNA: Yes, I will obey you. But you do not love me.

DURYODHANA: Drona, I order you to lead us.

DRONA: The wheel stops on me. It's my turn now. Yes, I will lead you. *At once, Duryodhana cries out in joy:*

DURYODHANA: Call the musicians! It's the last night of the war! *He goes.*

ASWATTHAMAN: Father, do you really know the way to destroy the Pandavas?

DRONA: Yes, I know it.

KARNA: I don't believe you. Sometimes I tell myself your science is just a lie, a dead leaf blown in on the wind.

DRONA: I know the way. The only way.

KARNA: Then speak, as I'm now under your command. What secret formation will you use tomorrow, when you draw up your armies?

DRONA: There's only one formation that can destroy the Pandavas. The disc. Rotating on itself, advancing remorselessly, it crushes everything in its way. No one knows how to break it open. No one, except Arjuna.

KARNA: If we can draw Arjuna away from the battle, will you guarantee us victory?

DRONA: Yes, I guarantee it.

ASWATTHAMAN: How can you draw him away?

DRONA: By a ruse. We must launch an attack from the north, just before the end of the night, an attack led by determined men. Sworn to die by thousands of millions. The Trigarttans, for example. A savage attack that no one but Arjuna could repel.

ASWATTHAMAN: But Bhima and the other brothers will fight us. How can we stop them?

DRONA: I know the man to stop them. His name is Jayadratha. *He calls.* Jayadratha! *Jayadratha enters.*

DRONA: Tomorrow I will need you. When the Pandavas attack, you will place yourself here, to stop them. *He indicates a position that he has drawn in the earth.*

JAYADRATHA: I lived for two years without eating, to obtain a favor from the gods. The power to stop the Pandavas once, only once. All, except Arjuna.

DRONA: Go and prepare. *Jayadratha leaves.*

ASWATTHAMAN: And who will beat Arjuna, when he returns?

DRONA: Karna said he could beat him.

ASWATTHAMAN: These men whom you formed, whom you trained and brought up, whom you said were amongst the most beautiful flowers of the earth—are you ready to trick and slaughter them? *Drona does not speak.*

KARNA: Your son has asked you a question. You don't answer? You said you loved the Pandavas, that you wished for their victory. Now you must organize their death. Is your loyalty and your commander's pride strong enough for this?

ASWATTHAMAN: What's your decision? *Duryodhana enters.*

DURYODHANA: Drona, the night is wearing thin. You are now master of all our lives. We await your orders. *They all leave, except Karna, who lies down to rest.*

# KUNTI AND KARNA

*From the surrounding darkness, a woman's voice calls.*

KUNTI: Karna . . . *He replies without getting up:*

KARNA: Who is there? *Kunti comes out of the shadow and draws near. She speaks softly.*

KUNTI: It's me, Kunti. I remember that day long ago when, in the middle of a tournament, you appeared, glowing, radiant, and you said: "I alone can conquer Arjuna, I alone in all the world." At that moment, a woman's heart throbbed in silence. She couldn't speak. Later, you swore, "One day I'll kill him."

KARNA: What do you want?

KUNTI: I've come to find you, to hold you by the hand, to take you with me. *Karna replies, as he slowly gets to his feet:*

KARNA: Your voice draws me deep into the past, back to my childhood; the sound of your voice . . . I feel a hand on my forehead. Is it a dream? Or simply the memory of a shattered truth? All my life I've heard rumors—my mother abandoned me, my mother abandoned me. Often, in my sleep, a veiled woman would come to me. Are you still a dream? Why does the mother of my enemies suddenly make me a child?

KUNTI: Come with me.

KARNA: Rage, hate, passion for victory—all seem false, like fevers at night. Where do you want to lead me?

KUNTI: Over there, to the other camp, toward those lights.

KARNA: Toward my enemies? Toward Arjuna?

KUNTI: Yes.

KARNA: And there I'll find my mother again?

KUNTI: Yes.

KARNA: She rejected me from the very first. She put me in a cradle, gave me over to a river. The cruelest enemy couldn't have done me so much harm. She never gave me a mother's tenderness, her warmth. Kunti, tonight, for the first time, you're concerned with me. Why?

KUNTI: I want to give you back your rights, your position.

KARNA: It's not true. You know that I intend to fight and you're afraid I'll kill Arjuna.

KUNTI: Karna, you are my son; you are my eldest son. You are born of me. Your mother asks your pardon—I was so young. Go and join Arjuna. When you are reunited, everything will be possible. Give me your hand, come with me toward the lights. *They walk a few paces together then Karna stops, turns back.*

KARNA: I am the son of a driver. What you have torn, nothing can repair. *They are silent a moment. Karna adds:* The day is bloody. Suddenly the night is almost peaceful; this sad adventure bursts my heart. Leave me alone, naked once again, on this great red river. Go. *She goes. He calls her back:* Kunti . . . *She stops.* I can do one thing for you. I will not kill Yudhishthira, I promise you. I will not kill Bhima, I promise you, nor the twins, sons of Madri. I will not kill them. I will only kill your son Arjuna; for one of us must die, him or I. In this way, after the battle, you will keep the same number of sons. *She looks at him for a moment.* Not another word. Go.

# THE DEATH OF ABHIMANYU

*In the morning, Arjuna and Krishna are hurriedly leaving for battle when a youth (Abhimanyu) places himself in front of them and says to Arjuna:*

ABHIMANYU: Father, where are you going?

ARJUNA: The Trigarttans have made a ferocious attack. I'm going to throw them back.

ABHIMANYU: Take me with you.

ARJUNA: Abhimanyu, you aren't old enough for war. We're going to swim in blood. *Abhimanyu stops his father.*

ABHIMANYU: I'm your son and I'm strong—as strong as you. Are you afraid you'll grow old in my shadow? Why leave me yawning in a tent, surrounded by women? I need to fight. Take me with you.

KRISHNA: Abhimanyu, your place is here! Out of the way.

*Krishna forces Abhimanyu to move aside and the two men leave. Abhimanyu remains alone. Draupadi enters and sees him.*

DRAUPADI: Abhimanyu, your mother and your young wife are looking for you. What are you doing here, dressed for war?

ABHIMANYU: I couldn't sleep. All night long my skin burned and my heart kept knocking on my chest. *There is a sound of distant warfare, drums. Draupadi looks ahead.*

DRAUPADI: The earth has vanished. There is only dust and men, a giant wheel of men grinding toward us. Abhimanyu, what is it?

ABHIMANYU: Drona has just launched his great offensive. *At this moment, Yudhishthira and Bhima appear, very agitated.*

YUDHISHTHIRA: Drona is advancing. He's in the center of his iron disc. He's crushing everything, he'll grind us to dust.

BHIMA: Our elephants panic, they're fleeing in every direction.

YUDHISHTHIRA: Listen, the disc is advancing on us like a machine bolted with rivets of death. Who can break it open?

DRAUPADI: Only Arjuna.

ABHIMANYU: No. I can do so, too. *Abhimanyu goes toward them.*

YUDHISHTHIRA: Abhimanyu . . . you know how to force the disc?

ABHIMANYU: Yes, I know how.

DRAUPADI: Arjuna gave you the secret?

ABHIMANYU: No, but before my birth, as I lay in Subhadra's belly, I heard my father speak of this secret.

DRAUPADI: And you remember what he said?

ABHIMANYU: Word for word.

YUDHISHTHIRA: Abhimanyu, we're lost. The disc will destroy us. Your father is far away. I appeal to you.

DRAUPADI: He's almost a child.

ABHIMANYU: Child I may be, but I'll attack Drona's iron wall. I'll crack it apart. Only, in my mother's womb I didn't hear all the secret.

DRAUPADI: What exactly did you hear?

ABHIMANYU: I heard how to force a way into the disc, but if the disc closes, I don't know how to come out.

YUDHISHTHIRA: Open up a breach, that's all we need; a breach and we'll follow you!

BHIMA: Open a breach, I'll be at your heels.

DRAUPADI: If you succeed, you'll be your father's equal.

YUDHISHTHIRA: Quick! The disc's approaching!

ABHIMANYU: Yes. I'll open a breach! Where's my driver? Bring me my arms! *As he says these words, his mother, Subhadra, runs up to him:*

SUBHADRA: What are you doing? Where are you going, my son? Why these weapons?

ABHIMANYU: Victory calls me. I'm going to fight.

SUBHADRA: You're going to fight? Why? Are all our men dead?

ABHIMANYU: The living need me. My family, the entire earth today needs me. Yudhishthira has asked for my support! Tie on my weapons! *A driver runs in. He helps Abhimanyu to prepare.*

SUBHADRA: Who is your enemy?

ABHIMANYU: You hear what's making the earth growl? That's my enemy!

SUBHADRA: The iron disc, commanded by Drona? Abhimanyu, your words are not your own, the thought of glory makes you blind. You forget your mother. Your death is here!

ABHIMANYU: Without me, it's death for everyone. But I know the special secret and I'll have miraculous powers. Don't be afraid, Mother, be proud and attentive. Watch how I walk. I'll lead the troops like a flame; all the armies will follow me! Arjuna is my father and the thought of him comes to my aid. Kiss me. *Abhimanyu kisses his mother and is ready for the battle.*

*The enemy army, formed like a disc and commanded by Drona, approaches. On seeing the child, Drona calls to him:*

DRONA: Abhimanyu, out of the way!

ABHIMANYU: Drona, I'm going to break open your disc. Your slaughter ends here! *The battle begins. Abhimanyu manages to force his way into the disc, breaking it apart.* Your disc is in pieces! The heads of your men will roll in the dust! *He fights vigorously, repulsing his opponents. Duryodhana cries furiously to Drona:*

DURYODHANA: All my army shattered by a child! Drona, where is your promise? Are you in love with our enemies, too? Dushassana, go ahead! *Dushassana obeys.* Kill this arrogant child! This lackey of death who smiles and despises us! Kill him! *Dushassana is in front of Abhimanyu.*

ABHIMANYU: I see you! My fist will crush you, Dushassana! Come nearer! *The two warriors fight violently. Dushassana is losing. He is wounded and carried off.* Take that! Fall! Who wants to die now? I blaze, I'm dancing with strength! Karna, I've killed your eldest son! Duryodhana, I've killed your eldest son! I fly between the armies! Follow me, I've opened the disc! Throw yourself into the breach! *Drona then calls:*

DRONA: Jayadratha! Where is Jayadratha? *Jayadratha appears at once.* Quickly, in position! This is your moment. Bar the Pandavas' way! *Jayadratha positions himself. Bhima and Yudhishthira surge forward but seem stopped by an irresistible force.*

ABHIMANYU: Bhima! Yudhishthira! Over here! You'd think the air itself is blocking you! Quick! Why are you hurling yourselves against a wall of air? *With their men, Duryodhana and Drona gradually surround Abhimanyu, while Jayadratha effortlessly keeps the Pandavas at bay. Abhimanyu, surrounded, is still fighting.* I'm alone in the middle of the disc! And the disc is closing again! They're all around me. Karna, Drona, Aswatthaman, they're all against me! Come closer! *The men move round him.*

KARNA: *To Drona* You seem fascinated by his extraordinary strength.

DRONA: Break his chariot! *Karna breaks Abhimanyu's chariot.*

KARNA: His chariot is broken.

DRONA: Break his bow!

KARNA: His bow is broken.

DRONA: Break his sword!

KARNA: His sword is broken!

ABHIMANYU: Drona, you've broken my sword. But I've still this enormous club which no two men can lift. *Abhimanyu fights a moment with the club. The warriors break it.*

KARNA: His club is broken! *Abhimanyu seizes the wheel from his chariot.*

ABHIMANYU: I've still got my chariot wheel. I'll crush you under this wheel!

DRONA: Karna, break the wheel! *Karna breaks the wheel. The young warrior still tries to defend himself but he is hit. He cries:*

ABHIMANYU: Father! *Then he stops moving. He falls to the ground. He is dead. Drona, Karna, Duryodhana, Dushassana, Aswatthaman all surround the child's body. They are quite still and they drop their weapons. Everything is quiet.*

    *Then Gandhari and Dhritarashtra appear, guided by Sanjaya. The boy is with them.*

GANDHARI: Is Abhimanyu dead?

SANJAYA: He's lying on the ground.

BOY: He looks surprised. *Gandhari kneels beside the body and says to Dhritarashtra:*

GANDHARI: He's like the wind when it dies down. Those who killed him let their weapons drop. They weep in silence and they say, "It's just a child lying on the ground. Was this our duty?"

*The Kaurava warriors withdraw in silence. The royal couple follows. Yudhishthira, Bhima, Subhadra, and Draupadi draw near the body.*

*In the silence, Arjuna appears, tired and wounded, led by Krishna. They come forward slowly.*

ARJUNA: No music, no one sings, and as they see me my men draw away, looking at the ground. Why am I greeted in silence? Krishna, my body's limp and it's not from fatigue. Normally my son, Abhimanyu, runs eagerly to meet me. . . . *He discovers Abhimanyu's body:* I see him. He's lying unprotected on the ground. He isn't breathing. *He touches his son's arm and chest.* Cruel wounds cover his body like bites. He fought, and he's dead. Who killed him? Why, Abhimanyu? I could never grow tired of seeing you. You thought of me at the last moment, you cried out "Father, help me!" But I didn't hear you. I was far away and they struck you to the ground. These heroes have killed a child. *He straightens and says to Krishna:* Krishna, you knew it and you said nothing. *Krishna does not reply.* Who sent him to his death?

YUDHISHTHIRA: I did.

BHIMA: Only he knew how to force the iron disc.

ARJUNA: Where is Vyasa?

SUBHADRA: Vyasa has abandoned us. We are alone and my son is dead. He was an idol to women, a theme for poets. . . .

DRAUPADI: He was bewitched by war.

ARJUNA: You didn't defend my son.

YUDHISHTHIRA: We were all behind him, he was leading us to victory, but Jayadratha barred our way.

ARJUNA: Jayadratha?

BHIMA: Yes, with you away he had the power to stop us—only once.

YUDHISHTHIRA: Impossible to break past him.

ARJUNA: You sent my son to his death.

DRAUPADI: They're telling you the truth. Jayadratha has turned all his hate toward us. He killed your son.

ARJUNA: Now, I make a vow. Tomorrow I will kill Jayadratha. I will kill him before sunset. If I don't keep this promise, I'll throw myself into the fire and I myself will join the world of the dead. *Jayadratha appears. He listens to Arjuna from a distance.* Gods and men, listen to me! What I say is true. Just as water is part of the sea, so Jayadratha already belongs to death. May my chariot be ready at dawn! *Abhimanyu is carried away. Arjuna stays with Krishna who says to him:*

KRISHNA: You have made a terrible promise.

ARJUNA: Yes, I know.

KRISHNA: Tomorrow Jayadratha will be solidly protected.

ARJUNA: He will have eleven armies all around him.

KRISHNA: If you don't keep your word, you must die. And they know it. Tomorrow every cry on the plain will be your life.

ARJUNA: Krishna, did you let my son die so as to push me deeper into the fight?

KRISHNA: I'm crossing the great era of darkness with you. This struggle is absolute. You and your brothers are the world's only light. Every moment, remember what I told you: if your heart breaks or closes up, if it becomes bitter, dark, or dry, the light will be lost.

Tonight you spoke in grief. Your promise opens you to death. No one is dearer to me than you. I'm in anguish.

ARJUNA: Advise me.

KRISHNA: I will go to my tent to think. Tonight, neither of us will be able to sleep. *Jayadratha goes to Duryodhana. He is very agitated.*

JAYADRATHA: Duryodhana, I'm leaving. Arjuna has sworn to kill me.

DURYODHANA: Yes, so my spies tell me.

JAYADRATHA: He said: "Jayadratha is already dead. I will kill him tomorrow, before the sun goes down." I'm afraid. I'm sweating, my legs shake.

DURYODHANA: But he also said, "If I don't kill him, I'll throw myself into the fire."

JAYADRATHA: Yes.

DURYODHANA: It's an extraordinary opportunity. Arjuna has allowed sorrow to get the better of him and tomorrow his pride will be his death. We will surround you like a living ring of armor.

JAYADRATHA: Terrible winds whirl in the plain; the mountains shake and the night sky burns. Arjuna has sworn my death!

DURYODHANA: I've prepared everything, everything. No one will come near you. I'm telling you the truth. Shake off your fears and rejoice like me, because Arjuna has brought about his own death. Tomorrow he'll enter the fire and victory will be ours. Jayadratha, I forbid you to leave me. *Drona adds sadly:*

DRONA: Yes, Everything is against Arjuna. *Dhritarashtra and Gandhari wake up. The boy and Sanjaya are with them.*

DHRITARASHTRA: Sanjaya!

SANJAYA: I am here.

DHRITARASHTRA: Is it light?

SANJAYA: Yes, dawn has come. Those who are going to die get up and eat.

DHRITARASHTRA: Gandhari, what day is it?

GANDHARI: The fourteenth day of the war. *Duryodhana's voice says:*

DURYODHANA: And the last. *He has just appeared, smiling, a rose in his hand. He pays his respects to his father and mother.*

GANDHARI: It's you, Duryodhana.

DURYODHANA: Yes, Mother, I'm bringing you a budding rose. Tonight the battle will be won.

GANDHARI: Is Jayadratha well protected?

DURYODHANA: He's surrounded by thousands of elephants, thousands of chariots, thousands of men. For his battle order today, Drona has chosen the needle. He himself is on the point of the needle. Nothing will resist him. This evening, prepare to celebrate our victory. *The sound of drums and shouts. Sanjaya cries out:*

SANJAYA: Arjuna has begun the attack! He's advancing like a whirlwind.

GANDHARI: What are those terrible cries?

SANJAYA: The painted monkey on his flag is shrieking. Arjuna has pierced the Cambodgean army. *Duryodhana dashes out to join the battle.*

DHRITARASHTRA: I feel the earth shake. Who's approaching? *Suddenly, Bhima looms up in front of the royal couple. He is armed and impressive.*

BHIMA: It's me, Bhima! *Dhritarashtra is frightened. He tries to hit Bhima but does not manage to touch him.*

DHRITARASHTRA: Bhima!

BHIMA: I won't strike you, I've come to tell you that I'm annihilating your family. I've killed five of your sons since dawn! Soon you'll be alone in the dark. *Bhima moves away.*

DHRITARASHTRA: He's gone?

SANJAYA: He's returned to the battle.

DHRITARASHTRA: My hope's draining away, hour after hour. My son will destroy my people.

GANDHARI: Don't put the blame on your son! You don't know what justice is. Your heart has deserted you and your political sense is weak. *They leave, guided by Sanjaya. Duryodhana and Drona suddenly find themselves face to face.*

DURYODHANA: Drona, your heart is with them, I know it. Arjuna is burning up my armies, and you, what are you doing? You live with us, but you love those we can never love. I've promised to defend Jayadratha and you are leading him to his death.

DRONA: I can't change my battle order. The game we're playing here knows no pity and the stake today is Jayadratha. I'm only thinking of him.

DURYODHANA: And the weapon that's worth all the weapons and whose secret you know?

DRONA: I haven't the right to use it and Arjuna possesses a superior weapon.

DURYODHANA: But if you strike first? *Karna appears at this moment, tired and wounded. He sits for a while.* Karna! Looking for shelter! Then who will stand by me? I have always said that Karna has no rival! But you give up! You withdraw! *Karna gets to his feet.*

KARNA: No! This is the final lull before victory! If we hold out till nightfall, then without fail Arjuna will enter the flames. *They organize Jayadratha's defense.*

*Arjuna appears. All his efforts fail against this defense. He is wounded and Krishna supports him.*

ARJUNA: Krishna, I'm losing all my blood. I've no more breath. For each man I kill, another takes his place. I can't beat Drona, the sun goes down, daylight fades. Jayadratha is still alive and I am sure to die.

KRISHNA: Find a last atom of strength. Stand up again!

ARJUNA: I can't stand.

KRISHNA: And the weapon that Shiva gave you?

ARJUNA: No, I don't want to devastate the earth. I'll die alone.

KRISHNA: I will come to your aid. Take your bow.

ARJUNA: What can you do?

KRISHNA: I will darken the sun. It's the moment. I will make it disappear. *Krishna holds out his hand and the sun's light disappears. The surprised Kauravas look at the sky then give shouts of victory.*

ARJUNA: It's not really night?

KRISHNA: No, not yet, but they believe it. You hear them shout in triumph? They think you haven't kept your promise; they're singing your death. Look, they're putting down their weapons, the living armor parts.

ARJUNA: Jayadratha lifts his face, he looks at the sky.

KRISHNA: No one thinks of defending him. Take your bow, pick an arrow, you know how to shoot in the dark. *Arjuna takes his bow and sets an arrow. He aims.* He's advancing unprotected. He smiles, he thinks he's saved. Cut off his head! *Arjuna releases his arrow.*

*Jayadratha falls. The shouts of joy cease at once. Dhritarashtra moves forward.*

DHRITARASHTRA: Why this brutal silence? *Krishna himself replies:*

KRISHNA: Jayadratha is dead.

GANDHARI: But isn't it already night?

KRISHNA: No, now I lift darkness from the sky. *He gestures and the light returns. He says to Dhritarashtra:* You can't see it, but the sun is still dazzling, the battle isn't over and your disappointed son weeps. *Krishna's gaze follows Arjuna.* Arjuna and Bhima return to their camp. Yudhishthira tells them, "Seeing you again brings me back to life." *The light fades again, more slowly, and Krishna continues:* And the sun sets for the second time.

# THE DEATH OF GHATOTKATCHA

*Around Duryodhana are gathered his principal chiefs: Karna, Dushassana, Drona, and his son, Aswatthaman.*

DURYODHANA: I watch the fall of kings and I see contempt rise in their place. Drona, I thought you were my pillar, but you've spared Arjuna because you love him. And I feel I'm loathed. I'm vicious, hypocritical, I'm sick with greed, even my friends say so. My ambition is dragging them to death.

DRONA: Once more you attack me in the presence of Karna and of my son Aswatthaman. This is my answer: the dice that Sakuni rolled were not true dice, they were our enemies' arrows. You didn't understand this language. How can you still hope for victory? Yes, we are dying, we are dying because of you. I know it too, my end is near.

DURYODHANA: Karna, I turn to you, as you are the only one not to hate me. Save me and save us all.

KARNA: You offer me the command? You take it away from Drona?

DURYODHANA: No, I ask you simply to fight; to fight with all your strength and to win.

KARNA: Yes, I'll fight.

DURYODHANA: I can put my life in your hands?

KARNA: I have my iron lance given to me by a god. This lance bears Arjuna's certain death.

DRONA: You boast all the time. Go and fight.

KARNA: Drona, you are old and feeble. All that you love is over there, on the other side, and in the depth of your heart you hope for defeat. *Aswatthaman springs toward Karna, weapon in hand.*

ASWATTHAMAN: You insult my father, I'll tear off your head. *Drona himself seizes his son and overcomes him.*

DRONA: Stop, Aswatthaman, throw down your weapon!

KARNA: *To Drona* Why not let him approach? Are you afraid for your son's life?

DURYODHANA: Karna, Aswatthaman, what madness is possessing you? If our unity breaks, if you abandon me, I'll no longer be worthy of our poets' songs. Without your promises of victory I would never have launched this war.

ASWATTHAMAN: You suspect us of being other than we are. We accept to die for you.

DURYODHANA: To battle, everyone!

ASWATTHAMAN: To battle? At night?

DURYODHANA: Take torches!

*The Kauravas go out. Only the royal couple, Sanjaya, and the boy remain. Kunti draws near.*

GANDHARI: It's you, Kunti?

KUNTI: Yes, it's me. I tread this damp earth all night long.

DHRITARASHTRA: What do we hear? What's this noise?

KUNTI: The never-ending roar of battle.

DHRITARASHTRA: They're even fighting at night?

KUNTI: In the dark, the blows are monstrous. The earth is covered with a bloody slime. They no longer recognize their friends; they kill them. They kill fugitives, they kill men already bleeding from their wounds, they fight with nails, teeth, tearing out hair, they kill with stones.

DHRITARASHTRA: They must be stopped! They must be told to respect the rules! Sanjaya, go and tell them!

KUNTI: Useless. They'll kill Sanjaya! Nothing can calm such chaos.

SANJAYA: They've put three torches on each elephant and five lamps on each chariot. The army lights up the night. Thousands and thousands of flames. The shining rises from the earth. It's as though the trees of a forest were covered with glittering flies.

GANDHARI: The earth is burning. It's like the last night of the world. *Arjuna, Krishna, and Yudhishthira appear—exhausted, alarmed—with torches.*

YUDHISHTHIRA: Krishna, Karna is going to destroy us. He seems to be everywhere. If a bush shakes I think he's there. My men don't even recognize their severed limbs; they're delirious, all my army is going mad.

KRISHNA: Yes, tonight Karna is walking savagely across the war.

YUDHISHTHIRA: These cries tear my heart. The smell makes me sick. I hate this war. It destroys the mind.

KRISHNA: Arjuna, where are you going?

ARJUNA: I'm returning to the fight. *Krishna holds him back.*

KRISHNA: No, I don't advise you to face Karna tonight. The iron spear he clasps in his hand is for you. He's been keeping it in reserve for you for a long time. It's a divine spear that cannot fail to kill.

YUDHISHTHIRA: What can save us?

KRISHNA: It's a trick of darkness we need. No one can stop Karna, except . . . *He stops as though struck by an idea.*

YUDHISHTHIRA: Who?

KRISHNA: I'm thinking of Ghatotkatcha, the son of Bhima and the Rakshasi. He swore that one day he would arise to save his father. *The words are scarcely spoken before Ghatotkatcha appears out of the dark.*

GHATOTKATCHA: Here I am. Where's my father?

KRISHNA: He's fighting, but he's wounded and threatened.

GHATOTKATCHA: Who's threatening him?

KRISHNA: Karna. Listen carefully, Ghatotkatcha, your valiant hour has come. You know magic weapons. No one other than you can stop the driver's son. Be worthy of your father and your uncles. Karna's power is terrifying, but it's not equal to yours. Demon of eclipses and illusions, you are your family's last defense. In the secret of darkness, offer Karna to the gods.

YUDHISHTHIRA: I will protect your rear.

GHATOTKATCHA: No. I'm enough for Karna. I will save my father and my human family. The earth will speak of my battle as long as there are men to hear. Step aside. I must prepare. *Ghatotkatcha starts his magic preparations as Dhritarashtra asks:*

DHRITARASHTRA: Describe Ghatotkatcha to me. *Ghatotkatcha replies:*

GHATOTKATCHA: My eyes are blood, my beard green, my mouth a gash like the gate of death. Cross-eyed, vast-bellied, sharp-toothed, I ride on a great eight-wheeled chariot, its black iron covered with bearskins, drawn by monster horses whose color is ever on the change. My flag is drenched in blood, it is crowned with a wreath of guts, and its pinnacle is a vulture, whose wings touch the sky. Night increases my power. Elephants piss with fear.

DHRITARASHTRA: And Karna, where is Karna? *Karna has just appeared opposite Ghatotkatcha.*

KARNA: Karna is here. He prepares to fight.

GHATOTKATCHA: The demon seizes a savage circle of steel. . . .

KARNA: Karna splinters it with a shower of arrows. *The fight begins in the night lit by torches.*

GHATOTKATCHA: You won't escape from my hands alive! I leap, I howl into the clouds. I call down a rain of trees, a hail of rocks. At one moment I have a hundred bellies, a hundred heads, then I shrink into a finger. Suddenly I drop down dead; my father's enemies shout with joy! But once again I'm borne aloft. I thunder with laughter. I grow, I'm measureless, I exceed all excess.

DHRITARASHTRA: And Karna! Where is Karna?

KARNA: Karna stays where he is. He shoots razor arrows, reptile arrows.

GHATOTKATCHA: But the demon opens his cavelike chops and, laughing, swallows the cloud of arrows! Then I become a mountain! From this mountain tumbles a cascade, an enormous cataract of arms.

GANDHARI: And what is Karna doing under this avalanche?

KARNA: Calmly, he takes an arrow, he fixes a celestial weapon—an astra—to it and the mountain explodes!

GHATOTKATCHA: Then Ghatotkatcha becomes a cloud of blood. . . .

KARNA: But Karna clears it away with the astra of wind.

GHATOTKATCHA: Ghatotkatcha dives toward the earth! The earth splits, he plunges in; even the gods can't see him anymore! Then he multiplies the ferocious animals, the fire-headed snakes, the iron-beaked birds, the twisted-jawed hyenas.

KARNA: Karna exterminates them all.

GHATOTKATCHA: This voice you hear has pledged your death! Has pledged your death! He now rains down a torrent of blood, streaked with lightning and meteors, a hurricane of axes and uprooted trees! Ghatotkatcha has reached the eye of the vortex of his frenzy. He is dripping with blood and sweat! Your son's armies are crushed, heads smashed, horses anatomized, elephants torn joint from joint. *Duryodhana and Dushassana, still sheltering, bring Karna's magic lance and say to him:*

DUSHASSANA: Karna, kill him! Kill him with your lance! Otherwise, he will destroy us all.

DHRITARASHTRA: No, he must save his lance for Arjuna, for he can use it only once, only once.

GANDHARI: What's he doing? Is he going to let his lance go?

DUSHASSANA: Quick! Kill him! Nothing can resist this vicious rain, men are dying by millions! Hurry!

DURYODHANA: If you hesitate for one more moment, we're lost! Quick! Even Drona's begging you!

DHRITARASHTRA: No! He must keep his lance!

SANJAYA: He lifts his arm, the lance gleams in the night, it streaks from his hand like a burning snake.

GANDHARI: What is Ghatotkatcha doing? *Ghatotkatcha sees the lance coming toward him.*

GHATOTKATCHA: He sees it, he recognizes it. He wants to flee, he's terrified, but the lance strikes him and pierces his heart. His heart explodes. The lance goes on to the end of the sky to vanish among the stars.

SANJAYA: Ghatotkatcha gives his last cry, he's forced to let go of his life. His body swells up, it's gigantic. He raises himself as high as he can in the air, then he crumbles, crushing thousands of warriors under his mountainous corpse. *Karna leaves with the Kauravas amidst shouts of joy. Ghatotkatcha collapses. Bhima rushes forward to take him in his arms.*

BHIMA: Ghatotkatcha, my son! *Hidimbi appears at the same time. She helps Bhima carry their son's body. They go out chanting as for a burial. Krishna seems joyful. He dances.*

ARJUNA: Why are you rejoicing? Ghatotkatcha is dead. Tonight we grieve, and you, you dance and laugh. Why?

KRISHNA: Ghatotkatcha has just killed Karna.

YUDHISHTHIRA: What are you saying?

KRISHNA: No one could resist Karna so long as this lance was in his hands. Now you can hurl him into the other world. Yes, Arjuna, you can kill him.

ARJUNA: Did you thrust Ghatotkatcha into the fight knowing he was going to die?

KRISHNA: Karna is like the sun. You can't fix your eyes on him, his arrows are his rays. But now he's reduced to the simple condition of a man. I think I know the way to kill him. Watch him carefully and when you see his chariot sink in the mud, then strike. Yes, Ghatotkatcha has saved you. To preserve your life, I sent him to his death. Tonight I'm breathing in joy. I was born to destroy the destroyers and I became your friend out of love for the world.

# THE DEATH OF DRONA

*Drona appears with his son, Aswatthaman.*

ASWATTHAMAN: The men are blind with fatigue. They fight as in a dream, their eyes shut, striking their own bodies, giving themselves wounds. Father, let's all sleep an hour here on the battlefield.

DRONA: Yes, let's sleep.

*Aswatthaman gives a sign to the distant army and lies down beside his father. A figure draws near to Drona and Aswatthaman, who leaps up, weapon in hand.*

ASWATTHAMAN: Halt! Don't go near my father!

VYASA: I am Vyasa.

ASWATTHAMAN: What are you looking for?

VYASA: I'm not looking for anything. I'm watching over your father in his last sleep.

ASWATTHAMAN: What are you telling me? Why do you wish to kill my father?

VYASA: I don't know why I speak, nor what shadows move my tongue. I make no decisions.

ASWATTHAMAN: Who will kill him? Tell me!

*Vyasa points to a red, menacing shadow, moving slowly in the distance.*

VYASA: You see that red shadow? It's a man, born from fire. His name is Dhristhadyumna. Your father knows him.

ASWATTHAMAN: No one can kill my father.

VYASA: And yet each time he sleeps, the red phantom enters his dream and it says to him: "It's for this that I am born. And you know it, because you are afraid."

ASWATTHAMAN: My father has no fear, not even in secret. He has never committed the slightest error. *The man with the face of blood has sat down next to Drona, who still sleeps.*

DHRISTHADYUMNA: He has committed the error that can destroy a life. Your father was a brahmin, without possessions, wretchedly poor. He couldn't even buy you milk.

ASWATTHAMAN: Yes, I remember.

DHRISTHADYUMNA: He was ashamed of his poverty and used all his force to become a terrible warrior, the hardest of men. He was born for peace, but chose war. That was his error. *The apparition disappears after a short, menacing dance. Drona wakes, sees his son and asks him:*

DRONA: Why don't you sleep?

ASWATTHAMAN: Father, why did you tell all those chiefs you are going to die? Aren't you he whom no one can defeat?

DRONA: Aswatthaman, this is the point of the needle and death's eye is fixed on me. *Duryodhana appears suddenly:*

DURYODHANA: Drona, why did you agree to rest? Why not follow your advantage?

DRONA: Because I'm tired, I'm old. I've often told you so.

DURYODHANA: Where is Karna?

DRONA: Worn out by his fight against the demon. He's been treated and now he's asleep.

DURYODHANA: Aswatthaman, I'm giving you the northern army. Your men are waiting. *Aswatthaman leaves quickly.* Drona, day breaks, the fight is yours. Take up your arms, Arjuna is coming this way. *The sound of the bow, Gandiva, is heard.*

DRONA: I know the sound of his bow. I'm ready for him. *Drona and Arjuna face each other. The single combat begins. When Arjuna strikes successfully, Drona congratulates him.*

YUDHISHTHIRA: Master against pupil!

BHIMA: It's the fight of my dreams! *Drona and Arjuna move away, they disappear from sight, still fighting.*

DRAUPADI: Arjuna will never kill the man who taught him everything.

BHIMA: Arjuna's weakening. He's backing away!

YUDHISHTHIRA: I'm losing all hope of beating Drona. *Arjuna returns to the Pandavas' camp to rest and bandage his wounds.* Drona must lay down his arms. Nothing can stand up to this ancient fury; he'll massacre everyone. He has become war itself. How can we make him lay down his arms?

KRISHNA: There's just one way. Drona's only son is his whole life. He must be told that Aswatthaman is dead. He'll be so discouraged, so desperate, that he'll drop his weapons.

ARJUNA: But Aswatthaman isn't dead. It'd be a lie.

KRISHNA: I know.

YUDHISHTHIRA: I don't agree. Find another way.

BHIMA: Wait. *Bhima grabs an enormous club and goes out. There is a loud thud. Bhima returns and says:* There. It's done. I've killed Aswatthaman.

ARJUNA: Whom?

BHIMA: Our elephant called Aswatthaman, I've killed him.

KRISHNA: You've an elephant called Aswatthaman?

BHIMA: Yes, and I've killed it. *He shouts toward the enemy lines:* Drona, can you hear me? Drona! *Drona's voice can be heard in the distance:*

DRONA: What do you want Bhima?

BHIMA: I've killed Aswatthaman! *Silence. Then Drona's voice asks:*

DRONA: Whom have you killed?

BHIMA: I've killed Aswatthaman! *Drona appears. Bhima says again:* Aswatthaman is dead.

DRONA: I can't believe my son is dead. I suspect a lie. Yudhishthira, you who can only tell the truth, I ask you: has Aswatthaman been killed?

*Yudhishthira hesitates.*

BHIMA: He doesn't believe me, answer him. *The red dancer appears at this point and takes several steps toward Drona who appears stunned at the sight of him.*

DRONA: Dhristhadyumna, why are you advancing on me? Has daybreak brought me my death? *To Yudhishthira:* Has Aswatthaman been killed? *Yudhishthira still refuses to lie. Dhristhadyumna moves slowly toward Drona.* Has Aswatthaman been killed, yes or no? *Yudhishthira decides to reply:*

YUDHISHTHIRA: Aswatthaman . . . *He lowers his voice and turns his head* the elephant . . . *He raises his voice again* has been killed. *A silence follows his words. Drona moves away and becomes motionless. Arjuna says to Yudhishthira:*

ARJUNA: Your greed for victory has corrupted you. You've slipped into a lie like the rest of mankind.

KRISHNA: From now on, he's part of the earth. Perhaps this weakness will bring him victory. Look at Drona, he would like to fight still, but he can't. *Drona seems unable to move. Bhima moves toward him.*

BHIMA: All at once, I see you clearly. You've no love in you. Your only love is killing, burying your iron deep in men's flesh. Your life is a long procession of corpses.

KRISHNA: Dhristhadyumna, strike quickly. You were born for this act. *Dhristhadyumna seems to hesitate as though still afraid of approaching Drona.* Don't be afraid, his energy is leaving him and you alone can take his life. *Dhristhadyumna, his sword drawn, moves toward Drona.*

ARJUNA: His death is inconceivable.

KRISHNA: His death is natural. Watch. His eyes are already closed, his breath quiets, it stops. *All eyes are on Drona.*

BHIMA: He's shining with light.

KRISHNA: He has reached the farthest fringe of life. His breath leaves him and rises into the air. This is what we see. Only his body stays. Dhristhadyumna will cut off a dead man's head. *Dhristhadyumna cuts off Drona's head and leaves shouting:*

DHRISTHADYUMNA: Drona is dead! Drona is dead! *Yudhishthira has fallen to the ground. Bhima, staring into the distance, says to the others:*

BHIMA: They scatter! They flee! Duryodhana tries to check the rout, but panic spreads.

DRAUPADI: *To Yudhishthira* Rise up! Rejoice!

ARJUNA: We've committed a crime. Victory is meaningless now.

YUDHISHTHIRA: Yes, I killed him with my lie.

DRAUPADI: I hear you calling our enemies' death a crime. I don't understand. Did Drona leap up to forbid Sakuni to cheat? And

Dushassana to drag me by the hair? I've endured shame and exile with you and you kept on repeating: "I'll destroy them, I'll destroy them."

BHIMA: And now you despise us; you sow glass in our wounds.

DRAUPADI: Listen. When Dushassana dragged me by the hair, he was dragging dharma. All my life I've heard wise people say, when dharma is protected, it protects. When it is destroyed, it destroys. Our enemies will be destroyed. Yes, you lied, your distress made you lie. But sometimes the only way to protect dharma is to forget it. Ask Krishna. He knows. *Suddenly Yudhishthira lifts his head and asks:*

YUDHISHTHIRA: What's that noise? *There is the sound of battle cries and music.* Their courage has returned. *Arjuna goes to survey the battlefield and announces:*

ARJUNA: Yes, they're advancing.

YUDHISHTHIRA: Who's leading them?

ARJUNA: Aswatthaman! He chases the deserters, he blocks their way, he calls them to order.

YUDHISHTHIRA: Quick!

*The Pandavas leave. Aswatthaman rushes forward, furious, accompanied by Duryodhana and Dushassana. They stop in front of Drona's bloody body.*

DURYODHANA: They've assassinated your father!

ASWATTHAMAN: His eyes were always fixed on death. I've no right to cry for him, but my angry body howls.

DURYODHANA: You couldn't defend him. You must take your revenge. *Aswatthaman says nothing. Duryodhana resumes:* Aswatthaman, I'm asking for the truth. Your father knew the secret of a weapon of extermination. Did he give you this secret?

ASWATTHAMAN: Yes.

DURYODHANA: This weapon is sacred. Do you possess it?

ASWATTHAMAN: My father's orders were to let it sleep for eternity. Even at the end of his life, he did not wish it used.

DURYODHANA: But your father is dead, killed by a lie.

ASWATTHAMAN: Arjuna has an even more terrible weapon, Pasupata. If I launch my weapon, he will unleash his.

DURYODHANA: Unless he's dead already.

ASWATTHAMAN: The secret of this weapon has never been revealed. It could pierce the heart of the world, it could even kill the gods.

DURYODHANA: They cut off your father's head.

ASWATTHAMAN: The earth shudders, the winds draw back in fear. Duryodhana, I will launch my weapon only once, with all my strength—I will extirpate my father's killers. All our men take cover! *Aswatthaman, Duryodhana, and their men go to take cover. Dhritarashtra cries out:*

DHRITARASHTRA: No! He mustn't launch that weapon! We'll all perish! Sanjaya, stop him!

SANJAYA: Too late, the weapon is launched! *The lights change. The horrified Pandavas appear on the battlefield with Krishna, Draupadi, and Subhadra. There is a burst of light.*

YUDHISHTHIRA: What's this flame that's devouring the world? Elephants are howling in terror, snakes are hurling themselves into the sky.

BHIMA: Aswatthaman has just released his father's sacred weapon.

YUDHISHTHIRA: What can we do? Men, animals, the earth itself—all are shriveling to ashes.

GANDHARI: I see a white heat.

BHIMA: *To Arjuna* Arjuna! You have Pasupata. Turn it against him, quick!

DRAUPADI: Exterminate them! Don't let one of them remain to rejoice over our death! *Arjuna, disturbed, asks Krishna:*

ARJUNA: Krishna . . .

KRISHNA: Lay down your weapons. Quick, lie on the ground, don't move, empty your minds, make a void. One mustn't resist this weapon, not even in thought. Otherwise it will hook on to you relentlessly, it will become more ferocious still. *They all lie down except Bhima, who straightens up and throws himself at the flame shouting:*

BHIMA: I can fight it, I can stop it!

KRISHNA: Bhima! Come back! *Bhima fights with all his force against the approaching flame but the more he fights, the more the weapon's strength increases. Dhritarashtra, Gandhari, and Sanjaya have stretched out on the ground. Krishna forces Bhima to lie down:* Bhima, throw down your weapons! Lie down, don't look at anything. Empty your mind and think of the time when you didn't exist. *They are all lying on the ground. The flame passes over without burning them. They don't move for a moment, then Krishna lifts his head and looks:* It's over, the flames die down. A calm wind rises. I hear a bird sing. *They all get up and embrace one another.* We're alive. *They leave the battlefield.*

# KARNA TAKES COMMAND

*Duryodhana appears on the battlefield accompanied by his brother Du-shassana, Karna, and Aswatthaman. They watch the sacred weapon vanish. Duryodhana asks Aswatthaman:*

DURYODHANA: Why did you fail?

DUSHASSANA: Order the weapon back and release it a second time!

ASWATTHAMAN: I can't. If I call it back again, it will return with our death.

DURYODHANA: Drona has betrayed me even in death. His sacred weapon is ruined; it's disintegrating uselessly in the great emptiness. Have you other weapons?

ASWATTHAMAN: I've only my ordinary weapons. Duryodhana, I don't understand: in the same instant I saw the earth burnt and saved, whole armies dead and alive. The ruin of the world, is it such a great thing, or is it nothing at all? *Duryodhana addresses Karna:*

DURYODHANA: Karna, your day has come. Bhishma and Drona have fallen, two old men who spared Arjuna—you said so yourself. But you, your hate is pure, your strength intact. Drive away our darkness.

KARNA: Are you clearly offering me the command?

DURYODHANA: Yes.

KARNA: Of all your armies?

DURYODHANA: You hesitate?

KARNA: Duryodhana, I've given you my life and at last you give me what I've been waiting for: danger of death. I thank you. Arjuna against me, I against Arjuna. I will only return in victory. But he has Krishna as his driver. Where can I find someone with his power? *At this moment, a man comes forward and asks Karna:*

SALYA: You're looking for a driver, Karna?

KARNA: Who are you?

SALYA: I'm King Salya.

KARNA: I don't need a king. I'm looking for a driver.

SALYA: All the horses in the world obey me. You won't find a better driver anywhere. I heard you say, "I am superior to Arjuna." Well, I am superior to Krishna.

KARNA: Krishna is sometimes guided by a force we can't understand. He is perhaps a form of Vishnu.

SALYA: But the gods share the world, just as men do. There are those who have seen Shiva fighting in the half-light of dawn, driving one army against the other.

KARNA: Shiva only wishes to destroy. He gave Arjuna the final weapon.

DURYODHANA: You too, Karna, you too know its secret. Shiva's forms elude us, his desires escape our understanding. Oppose the subtle with the even subtler and the dark with darker still.

SALYA: Entrust me with your horses and I can make you win the battle.

DURYODHANA: Have the whole army assembled the moment the sun rises. See that everything is prepared.

*Duryodhana, Dushassana, Aswatthaman leave. Only Salya and Karna remain. They prepare the chariot for the fight. After several moments silence, Salya says:*

SALYA: Aren't you afraid?

KARNA: No one can ever say: "I'll see the sun rise tomorrow." Nothing in this world is lasting and you are going to drive me toward my destiny. But I alone can defeat Arjuna.

SALYA: You boast and brag, but you're deceiving yourself. No one can defeat Arjuna.

KARNA: I'll give whoever places Arjuna before me gold, villages, dancing girls.

SALYA: He'll be before you soon enough. Why waste your fortune? At this very moment his weapons are being prepared. He is calm. His brothers and Draupadi are with him. His father, Indra, watches him secretly and listens. Krishna is waiting. And you? Who's supporting you? Who wants your victory? Karna, your time is up. Can't you feel it?

KARNA: You just said, "I can make you win the battle."

SALYA: What deceptive battle are you fighting? Who do you think is your enemy? Nobody's bastard, haven't you a single friend to open up your eyes? You're a poor, miserable jackal howling at a lion, a frog in a monsoon bawling itself blue.

KARNA: Why get under my skin? Why needle away my courage? Are you my enemy? I know Arjuna better than you. I know who he is. I'm not a brainless insect throwing itself into a fire. I know what I'm doing. Look at this spear, shaped like a snake, full of venom. It could even pierce a mountain. With this spear I'll kill Arjuna, after which I'll open up your stomach, malicious idiot, trying to make me afraid. *A silence. Salya prepares the weapons, the harness, the chariot. Karna is immobile.*

SALYA: What are you thinking about?

KARNA: A curse.

SALYA: The one made by Parashurama, the man with the axe?

KARNA: How do you know?

SALYA: I heard the story of the worm that pierced your thigh; how you resisted the pain so as not to wake Parashurama, who was asleep.

KARNA: When he woke, he burst with anger and cried: "You lied to me about who you are! At the moment of your death, you will lose your memory and suddenly you'll forget the secret I taught you."

SALYA: Have you forgotten it? *Karna is silent for a moment. His lips move.*

KARNA: No, not yet.

SALYA: The worm in your thigh was probably some god trying to protect Arjuna.

KARNA: Irresistible, incomparable Arjuna. You are coming toward me with your extraordinary weapons, with your godlike hands. But I will kill you. I will lift your head from your body. I will kill you.

SALYA: If you are so sure of killing him, why are you afraid?

KARNA: Salya, or whoever you are, I'm shrouded in omens, menaced by darkness. Another time, walking in the country, I accidentally killed a brahmin's cow. He also cursed me. He shouted: "The moment fear enters your flesh, your chariot wheel will plunge into the earth." I can't get this ambiguous phrase out of my head. Yes, I think I am afraid. *A bell rings. Karna rouses himself and says:* The troops are assembled. Day is breaking. The moment has come. *Karna, driven by Salya, engages the battle.*

   *Dhritarashtra reappears with Gandhari, Sanjaya, Kunti.*

   *Karna and Yudhishthira are face to face. They fight a moment and Karna laughs, easily parrying Yudhishthira's blows. Then he disarms him. Yudhishthira tries to flee but Karna follows him and threatens him with his spear:*

KARNA: You want to run away? You wish to save your life? *Yudhish-thira does not reply. He is on the ground.* Don't be afraid. I promised your mother not to kill you. Go and hide and keep away from the fight. Get someone to sew up your dress and don't play at war with real men. *Karna goes with Salya to continue the battle elsewhere. Yud-hishthira, wounded and shamed, returns to his camp. Draupadi tends his wounds. In the distance, the furious sounds of battle can be heard. Yud-hishthira is delirious.*

YUDHISHTHIRA: Is Karna here?

DRAUPADI: Rest.

YUDHISHTHIRA: Where is he? Where's Karna?

DRAUPADI: Arjuna is hunting him down and Bhima is fighting As-watthaman.

YUDHISHTHIRA: Spread the word. Everyone must be told I'm not dead. What's the time?

DRAUPADI: Midday.

YUDHISHTHIRA: My life is a frozen field. . . . Ignorance is ice and truth throws no shadow. . . . I'm a toy in Karna's hand. . . . This forest sucks me dry.

DRAUPADI: Hush.

YUDHISHTHIRA: We must harvest the seeds of war and destroy them. Go, give the order. *He sits up.* Who's there?

DRAUPADI: Arjuna.

YUDHISHTHIRA: Arjuna returns?

DRAUPADI: Yes.

YUDHISHTHIRA: If Arjuna quits the battle, Karna is dead. *Arjuna returns with Krishna. They are exhausted. As soon as he sees them, Yud-*

*bishthira says to Arjuna, talking very quickly:* Arjuna, come here. Describe Karna's death. I can talk about it now. For fourteen years, every night I thought of Karna, I sweated with fear and shook with hatred. Awake, asleep, I saw Karna everywhere—in the gardens, in my room, by the river, wherever I went I saw him. Karna filled the universe. Today he caught me and I fled. Sit down. Tell me in detail how you killed him.

ARJUNA: Karna is not dead. No one can kill him. He's like a mad blaze that devours everything in its path and he draws fresh heat from the midday sun. No, I haven't killed Karna and even Bhima is in danger.

YUDHISHTHIRA: You haven't killed Karna and you return? You abandon your brother? But you always said to me, always, "I will lead the war and I will kill Karna. I swear it. I am born to kill him." And I believed you. Yet, when the moment comes, you betray me. The world's greatest archer, the legendary conqueror whom none can eclipse. With what horses! What prodigious weapons! And Krishna himself as driver, what more could you need? If you yield to Karna, if you are a coward, give your bow to someone else! And go! Better never to have been born, or born in the sixth month, an abortion, than to end as a deserter, panting with fear. *Furious, Arjuna grabs his sword and hurls himself at his brother. Krishna and Draupadi hold him back.*

DRAUPADI: Arjuna!

ARJUNA: I'll kill you!

KRISHNA: Quiet! Calm down! I can see no one here you should kill.

ARJUNA: Whoever calls me a coward, whoever says to me, give your bow to another, I'll kill him, I tell you, I'll kill him.

KRISHNA: You are lost. You no longer know what you're doing. How can you say "I'll kill my brother"?

ARJUNA: He wished me dead before I was born. He's no longer my brother.

KRISHNA: He's suffering, delirious. Karna frightened him and he's wounded.

DRAUPADI: He says Karna can only be eliminated by you. With Karna gone, the battle would come to an end. *Arjuna addresses Yudhishthira:*

ARJUNA: Don't reproach me for anything, you who always keep well out of harm's way. Bhima could reproach me, yes. He's out there, on a mountain of corpses. But you, you are cold, you live in terror, your heart is hard. I've given you everything and you insult me, lying in Draupadi's arms. You are cruel, you wear a mask. No good to me has ever come from you. It's you who played at dice, you who lost everything; the origin of the disaster is you. You hide, but you are devoured by your dream of perfection. You are ready to sacrifice everything—yes, our lives and all the lives around you—so that you can be the purest of all men.

KRISHNA: Your sword is still in your hand. Whom do you wish to kill?

ARJUNA: I wish to kill myself.

KRISHNA: Do you know who you are? Do you know whom you might kill? *Arjuna is silent a moment before replying:*

ARJUNA: Yes, I know who I am.

KRISHNA: At this moment, it's not only your life that's at stake. The whole earth is watching your sword. *Arjuna calms down and says to Yudhishthira:*

ARJUNA: Forgive me. I'll join Bhima. Today I'll kill Karna. *He wants to leave, but Yudhishthira calls him back:*

YUDHISHTHIRA: Arjuna, all that you've said is true. You must now break your allegiance and turn your back on me. Bhima will make a very good king.

KRISHNA: No. You must stay firm.

DRAUPADI: You heard Arjuna's promise. Before the day ends, he will send Karna to his final rest.

KRISHNA: The war draws to its close.

DRAUPADI: And you are the winner. *Arjuna bows before Yudhishthira.*

ARJUNA: Forgive me and stay. I beg you.

YUDHISHTHIRA: *To Arjuna* If you don't kill him today, you destroy my life.

ARJUNA: I will kill him. *To Krishna* Guided by you. *Yudhishthira seems very tired. Krishna says to Draupadi:*

KRISHNA: Take him away and give him good care. *Draupadi helps Yudhishthira to leave. Krishna and Arjuna watch them go and Krishna says to Arjuna:* Where would you be now if you had killed your brother and your king? What pain! What hell!

ARJUNA: For a moment, I could have killed him.

KRISHNA: So I saw.

ARJUNA: I have sworn Karna's death.

KRISHNA: Yes, the long-awaited day is here. Karna will rise before you, ablaze, steaming with blood, fighting mad.

ARJUNA: Am I really stronger than he is?

KRISHNA: If you are afraid of him, don't despise him. See him as he is.

ARJUNA: I don't despise him. I'm wet with fear. Krishna, who is Karna? You must tell me.

KRISHNA: I will tell you now. Karna's father is the sun.

ARJUNA: I'm lost. Nothing can outshine the sun.

KRISHNA: You asked me, "Am I stronger than he?" It's a false question. It's not your strength against his. It's one immense force against another, because we have, I think, secret allies. Don't give in to despair. You are not alone.

ARJUNA: Let's get my chariot ready. Stay with me. *They leave together.*

# DUSHASSANA'S DEATH
# KARNA'S DEATH

*Vyasa reappears. The boy calls to him and catches up with him.*

BOY: Vyasa, I'm very tired.

VYASA: Let's sit down.

BOY: Will the war end one day?

VYASA: Yes, it will end.

BOY: I'm afraid. I thought I was going to die when Aswatthaman launched his weapon.

VYASA: So did I.

BOY: But you told me: "I'm the author of this poem." Could your poem kill you? *Before Vyasa can reply, Bhima staggers in, covered in blood and mud.*

BHIMA: Vyasa, is it you?

VYASA: Yes, Bhima.

BHIMA: My eyes are streaming with blood, all my body is mashed and mangled, I'm nothing but holes.

BOY: Where've you been?

BHIMA: I haven't stopped fighting for three days. Now I'm ready to drop. Vyasa, I'd like to plunge into a river and let the clear current wash my blood.

Vyasa: Arjuna is going to fight against Karna. This is the fateful day.

Bhima: Where are we?

Vyasa: The battle has mixed up everything. The killing is chaotic.

Bhima: Vyasa, I'm finished. If you're still in charge, why are you forcing us to die?

Vyasa: Bhima, if I stop the war now, where would be the victory? *Vyasa and the boy build a sort of shelter for Bhima.* Take shelter here and rest. *Dushassana appears suddenly, axe in hand.*

Bhima: Who's coming toward me? My eyes are full of blood. I can only see a moving shape.

Dushassana: It's me.

Bhima: Who, you? Bring your body over here.

Dushassana: Try to see who I am. It's Dushassana!

Bhima: Dushassana! They've told you I've been wounded and you're coming on tiptoe to kill me. *Dushassana knocks down Bhima's shelter and pushes away his club.*

Dushassana: Can't you get up anymore?

Bhima: No, I'm so tired I'm falling apart. I'm blind and I'm talking in my sleep. *Dhritarashtra and Gandhari have drawn near. Gandhari calls out to her son:*

Gandhari: Dushassana, what's brought you here? Don't go near him! *Dushassana ignores his mother's advice.*

Dushassana: You're slow and heavy. I'm not afraid of you.

Bhima: I'm heavy with dead men's blood. *Dushassana seizes his axe and strikes. Bhima avoids the blows as best he can.* Spare me, I'm defenseless. . . .

DUSHASSANA: I'm going to save myself and save my brothers! *Dushassana dances lightly around Bhima. He hits and wounds him. Bhima clutches his wounded arm.*

BHIMA: You touched me, your friends will be happy. *Dhritarashtra shouts to his son:*

DHRITARASHTRA: Keep away, Dushassana!

DUSHASSANA: *To Bhima* You sweat like an old elephant and you can't move anymore. Think of your life which ends here!

BHIMA: Dushassana . . . *Suddenly, as Dushassana is about to deliver a mortal blow, Bhima relaxes. His hand shoots out and grabs his opponent's ankle. Dushassana falls. Bhima pounces and overcomes him.* Miserable abortion, who do you want to kill? *Dushassana struggles, thrashes about wildly in all directions.*

DUSHASSANA: Help!

BHIMA: Stop crying! Your black hour has come, Dushassana. This is where it all ends! Now! *He raises his voice and calls:* Draupadi! Can you hear me? Come! *Draupadi appears.* Look! I will drink his blood, just as I promised. It's your turn, Dushassana. You've a gasp or two still left. Think back over your wretched life and remember Draupadi drawn by the hair. Look at her. Let her be the last thing you see. *He forces Dushassana to face Draupadi.*

DUSHASSANA: My brothers! Save me! Where is Karna? Karna!

BHIMA: Karna can't hear you. There's no one to help you. And I rip out your life. Go. Enough. Die. *He plunges his hands into Dushassana's belly and kills him. Then he crouches down to drink his blood and eat his entrails, fulfilling his promise.* Hmm . . . my enemy's blood is more delicious than my mother's milk, better than honey, than wine, sweeter than the sweetest drink on earth. *Dushassana dies in horror, as he watches Bhima eat his intestines. Draupadi turns away abruptly.* Draupadi, don't go away! Watch what I'm doing for you! You can wash your hair now. *He looks around.* Don't look at me in horror, through half-closed eyes; don't mutter through your teeth "this one isn't human." I suck his life's blood from his guts. And he beseeched me to drink it. He begged for death, he humiliated our wife. He made fun of me. He danced over me, crying, "The great ox! The great ox! The beast!" Now it's my turn to dance! *He stands up, covered in blood, and dances around the corpse. His dance makes the earth shake. He looks at Dushassana for the last time and says to him:* We weren't born to be happy. Farewell. *He leaves in silence, leaning on Draupadi.*

*Duryodhana and Gandhari are by Dushassana's body. Gandhari touches Duryodhana and asks him:*

GANDHARI: Duryodhana, will you spare me just one son? *Aswatthaman appears.*

ASWATTHAMAN: Enough murder. Enough blood. Stop the war today.

DURYODHANA: Bhima has torn out my brother's guts and you want me to stop the war? Karna! *Dhritarashtra and Gandhari carry off Dushassana's body as Duryodhana says to Aswatthaman:* All my spies tell me their men are tottering with fatigue. Even Arjuna can hardly stand. Karna's well rested. Disaster is changing its course, it's turning back on our enemies. How can you tell me to give up, you who tried to wipe out everything with your giant flame? You whose father was killed by a lie? *Karna arrives ready for battle, attended by Salya.* Karna, this is the moment. All our lives are in your hands.

ASWATTHAMAN: Here is Arjuna. *Arjuna appears, driven by Krishna. Draupadi and Yudhishthira stay in the background. Karna and Arjuna are face to face. A moment's silence. Karna says to Arjuna:*

KARNA: Here I am, Arjuna. I, the bastard, the obscure; you, the prince, the conqueror. But the sky has opened up for me and the sun fills me with strength. You won't end this day alive. *Arjuna does not reply and, at a signal from Krishna, is the first to attack. Karna laughs, easily parrying the first blows. Suddenly Kunti rushes in, crying:*

KUNTI: Stop them! Stop them from fighting one another! *Vyasa prevents her from intervening.*

VYASA: Kunti, go back. One of them must die. You know it.

KUNTI: Why? Who said so? Who needs this death? Stop them, Vyasa, they don't know who they are.

GANDHARI: Who are they? Kunti, tell me!

KUNTI: They are, they are . . .

KARNA: Kunti! *Karna motions to Kunti. She is silent and withdraws. The combat resumes. It becomes more and more furious. Suddenly Arjuna wounds Karna. He falls but gets up immediately, laughing. In turn, he strikes Arjuna. Krishna and Salya direct and assist the two combatants. Karna breaks Arjuna's chariot; his victory seems assured. Suddenly he stops as though paralyzed. His chariot does not move despite his and Salya's efforts. A cry rises from the warriors.*

GANDHARI: What's this cry? What can you see?

SANJAYA: Karna's chariot wheel has just plunged into the earth. He can't go on. *Karna, suddenly helpless, cries to Arjuna:*

KARNA: Wait! Wait until I free my wheel! You haven't the right to strike, you know it. *Arjuna, respectful of the rules, stops. But Krishna urges him to attack.*

KRISHNA: Strike! This is the moment! Don't listen to him! Don't wait! *Karna endeavors to free his wheel while saying to Arjuna, who still does not move:*

KARNA: I stand before you unarmed, threatened, weak. Law and honor protect me. Let me free my wheel. *It is Krishna who answers him:*

KRISHNA: You speak of honor now, but when Sakuni threw the dice, where was your honor? What hole did you hide it in? Don't scorch your mouth with that word; you won't escape alive. *He's crying with anger, he's yours. Salya comes between Arjuna and Karna.*

SALYA: A chariot wheel doesn't stick without reason. Who's caught hold of this wheel? Who is playing this final trick?

KRISHNA: *To Arjuna* I'll tell you who's caught hold of this wheel: it's the earth herself with her muddy hands. Suddenly she's taking part in the battle. She's defending herself and she's come to your aid. It's she who's grasping his chariot wheel and she won't let go. Strike! Yes, finish the war! *Just as Arjuna lifts his weapon, Salya says to Karna with great urgency:*

SALYA: Karna, don't let yourself be killed like a driver! Rise up. Call your irresistible weapon and release it. This is the moment! Quick!

DURYODHANA: Yes, Karna, refuse to die!

SALYA: Launch the final weapon! *Karna looks at the sky.*

KARNA: I know the secret formula. If I pronounce it, a heavenly creature will come and place the weapon in my hand. *Krishna tries very hard to make Arjuna strike:*

KRISHNA: What's paralyzing you? Strike! *Salya pushes Karna to call up the final weapon:*

SALYA: Call! Say the words! Save us all!

KARNA: Yes, I call, I call this distant creature . . . *He holds out his hand, open as though to receive the weapon* and I say to her . . . *Suddenly his voice stops, his mouth half-open.*

DURYODHANA: What's happening? Speak!

KARNA: What do I have to say? *Deeply troubled, Karna searches for lost words:* It was a simple phrase. Suddenly I don't remember it any more. . . . Why has the sun fled? What's this shadow? *Nobody answers.* My wheel is buried in the mud, my head is dark, and an ancient mystery kills me. *What do I have to say? Krishna then says to Arjuna, this time without violence:*

KRISHNA: All the signs are against him. Take his life. *Arjuna kills Karna who no longer defends himself. Duryodhana collapses in a faint.*

# DURYODHANA'S DEATH
# THE END OF THE WAR

*A moment's silence. Kunti has also fainted. The Pandavas leave. Gandhari stands and takes a few steps.*

DHRITARASHTRA: Gandhari, where are you going?

GANDHARI: I want to touch my son and speak to him. Vyasa, show me the way. *Vyasa takes Gandhari's hand and leads her to Duryodhana. He comes to and sees Karna's body.* My son . . .

DURYODHANA: Karna, your look still imposes fear, your cold mouth seems ready to command.

GANDHARI: My son . . .

DURYODHANA: When you asked him for anything, he always answered: "Yes, here it is." He didn't know how not to give. Lifeless, glorious man . . .

GANDHARI: Everything bleeds, everything weeps, stop this war. Yudhishthira will have pity on you and you can live in peace.

DURYODHANA: Yudhishthira will never forgive me. He and his brothers will track me as far as the abyss where the world ends. I will not live like a puppet king. I must enter the last, the harshest part of my journey. *He stands up and prepares for the fight.*

GANDHARI: Your brothers are cold, your shattered troops desert. The rout has emptied your camp, everyone thinks you're already dead.

DURYODHANA: I call my last warriors—wounded, bleeding—I call them. *As though seeing warriors rise, ghostlike, he exhorts them:* Rise from the ground, gather your broken weapons, surround me for the last time. We are going to fight. *He kisses Karna and goes out. Dhritarashtra calls:*

DHRITARASHTRA: Sanjaya?

SANJAYA: I am here. *They go to Karna's body.*

DHRITARASHTRA: My heart must be made of stone, not to have broken by now. Help me carry Karna's body. *Dhritarashtra, groping, takes the body under the shoulders and Sanjaya takes the legs. They leave. Gandhari goes with them.*

   *Kunti remains unconscious on the ground.*

   *Vyasa and the boy reappear holding a light, brilliant cloth to suggest water. Duryodhana stretches out under the cloth with his club. At this moment, two hunters with bows enter hurriedly. They seem to look for something.*

FIRST HUNTER: This way, softly, come . . . *The second hunter moves forward.*

SECOND HUNTER: There are always ducks on this lake. Creep over to the other side. Not a sound. *The two hunters go cautiously to the edge of the lake. Duryodhana begins to sing.* Do you hear? It's like a voice speaking from the bottom of the lake.

FIRST HUNTER: What's the voice saying?

SECOND HUNTER: It's singing. It's bewailing a lost kingdom. It's Duryodhana's voice, he's there!

FIRST HUNTER: Can you see him?

SECOND HUNTER: Yes, there! Touch the water, it's hard and cold as stone. *Yudhishthira appears, accompanied by Arjuna, Bhima, and Krishna. He is injured and leaning on Draupadi.*

YUDHISHTHIRA: What's the name of this lake?

SECOND HUNTER: Dvaipayana.

YUDHISHTHIRA: And the water's hardened?

SECOND HUNTER: Yes, like transparent rock. Feel it. *Yudhishthira kneels at the edge of the lake, touches the hardened water and calls:*

YUDHISHTHIRA: Duryodhana! Are you there? *No reply. Krishna leans over the surface of the water.*

KRISHNA: Yes, he is there, I see him. He's there with his club.

YUDHISHTHIRA: He passed through the water?

KRISHNA: Yes, by magic. The waters opened and let him in, then he made them hard. No one could break them now.

YUDHISHTHIRA: Duryodhana? Do you hear me? *No reply.* Can you hear me? *Duryodhana's voice replies:*

DURYODHANA: Don't disturb my peace. I'm resting.

YUDHISHTHIRA: What are you doing in these icy waters? Get up, leave your conjuring, come out and fight.

DURYODHANA: My body is weary. I need to rest.

YUDHISHTHIRA: You'll have all the rest you need after the fight.

DURYODHANA: Tomorrow; I'll fight tomorrow. I want to stay here all night and sing.

YUDHISHTHIRA: You're afraid? *Duryodhana waits a moment before replying.*

DURYODHANA: Does it surprise you that fear can soak into a man? No, it's not fear that's drawn me into this lake, it's fatigue. It's good down here in the clear, clean water. I give you this earth, ruined, clothed in corpses. All I want is to wrap myself in an animal skin and disappear into the woods.

YUDHISHTHIRA: The earth you give me isn't yours. The bodies that cover it have been butchered by your greed. You respected your greed more than all these lives. Now, it's your life I want.

DURYODHANA: Very well, I'll come out. I accept the challenge to break through the waters and fight—but one against one.

YUDHISHTHIRA: You're a Kshatriya. You are entitled to fight according to our rules. Come out of the lake.

DURYODHANA: Can I choose my weapon?

YUDHISHTHIRA: Choose your adversary and your weapon! *Krishna then says to Yudhishthira:*

KRISHNA: Why take the risk? I can hear him puffing and swelling like a serpent.

DURYODHANA: I choose clubs! *Duryodhana suddenly springs from the lake, club in hand.*

KRISHNA: *To Yudhishthira* What will you do? He's been training with clubs every day for thirteen years. Every day! Against an iron statue! *Bhima then comes forward and says:*

BHIMA: I will fight you and I'll finish the war today. I will put an end to your life.

DURYODHANA: Come nearer! *Bhima goes up to Duryodhana and the two men begin to fight ferociously. Bhima tries to strike his adversary but Duryodhana skillfully avoids his attacks and strikes in return. He turns around Bhima, who is injured and moving heavily. Suddenly, after a feint, Duryodhana strikes Bhima who staggers and falls. Instead of killing him, Duryodhana says:* You're heavy, you can't keep up any longer. I could smash your skull, but one doesn't strike a fallen adversary. Get to your feet! *Krishna and Arjuna help Bhima up while Duryodhana moves away to regain his breath.*

KRISHNA: Are you wounded?

BHIMA: Yes.

KRISHNA: Badly?

BHIMA: Yes.

KRISHNA: Don't show it. Stay on your feet, you must convince him you're strong. Attack and aim low, hit his legs.

BHIMA: His legs? I can't, it's not allowed.

KRISHNA: I said hit his legs!

DRAUPADI: Break his thigh!

*Bhima returns to the fight. Duryodhana is as skillful as before and Bhima's club strikes the air. In a last effort, Bhima swings round and suddenly throws his club at Duryodhana's legs. Duryodhana screams and falls, his thighs smashed. Bhima crushes his head with his foot.*

YUDHISHTHIRA: *To Bhima* Bhima, take away your foot! This man has the same blood as you and he was a king. The war is over. Don't insult him. *In pain, Duryodhana calls Yudhishthira:*

DURYODHANA: Yudhishthira, listen to me, come. . . .

YUDHISHTHIRA: What do you want?

DURYODHANA: I've been hit, shamefully, on the legs, against all the rules. *Krishna intervenes at once. He wants to draw Yudhishthira aside:*

KRISHNA: Come, he's neither a friend nor an enemy. You don't waste tears on a block of wood. Let's go.

DURYODHANA: Krishna! You advised Bhima to aim at my legs. Do you think I didn't hear? You are the origin of evil! Sikhandin—that was your idea! And who tricked the sun? And the lie: Aswatthaman is dead? And who threw Ghatotkatcha against us to force Karna to give up his lance? And when Karna's wheel stuck in the mud, you said to Arjuna, "Take his life!" You! Always you! Death's cunning slave!

KRISHNA: All that you say is false and your only assassin is yourself. *To Yudhishthira* Your victory is complete. Let's go and celebrate.

DURYODHANA: Yes, go your way, stay in this unhappy world, I'm going to another world. Who is happier than I? I reigned on earth, I was just. I laughed, I sang, I loved my friends and my wives, I protected my servants, I held out my hand to the afflicted, I knew all human joys. Go and eat and dance. Go.

KRISHNA: No good man is entirely good. No bad man is entirely bad. I salute you, Duryodhana. I don't find any pleasure in your suffering. But your defeat is a joy. *Duryodhana stays alone, clinging to life as night draws near. Aswatthaman approaches him. In the distance, songs and music.*

ASWATTHAMAN: Your enemies are singing their victory. Can you hear them? *Duryodhana lifts himself onto his elbow.*

DURYODHANA: Aswatthaman . . . *Aswatthaman supports him and listens.* The five brothers won't stay in the camp tonight. They've already left. The others will drink, drink, then they'll sleep heavily, sleep. . . . *Aswatthaman has understood. He stands up briskly and leaves. Krishna then appears. He goes to Kunti who is still unconscious.*

KRISHNA: Kunti, get to your feet. Your sons are waiting for you in the town. *Kunti comes to. Krishna helps her stand up and walk.*

KUNTI: The night is not yet over?

KRISHNA: No, not yet.

KUNTI: Krishna, somewhere in my heart I'm uneasy, as though death hasn't yet finished its work. *At this moment in the distance, the festive music stops. Kunti and Krishna do not move. They are troubled.* The feast is over.

KRISHNA: The victors sleep.

KUNTI: Who of the Kauravas is still alive?

KRISHNA: Duryodhana isn't yet dead.

KUNTI: And who else?

KRISHNA: Aswatthaman's escaped. Death is at work in him and he can't rest.

KUNTI: Krishna, we must find them. It's not a victorious silence. *Krishna leaves quickly. Kunti follows him. Then Aswatthaman appears holding a bloody sword. He goes to Duryodhana still lying on the ground in the night.*

ASWATTHAMAN: If you still have breath, listen to me. . . . *Duryodhana lifts himself and listens.* When I left you, I hid in the forest and there, in the darkness of a vast tree, I saw an owl, ruthlessly exterminating baby crows in their sleep. I said to myself, my hour has come. As I approached the camp, brutally, an enormous being burst from the earth, a creature of horror spitting fire, sweating blood, crying, "You won't enter! You won't enter the camp!" The colossus had a thousand jaws, a thousand arms whirling fire and steel. I tried to fight him, but this monster phantom was a barrier I couldn't cross. Then I realized that what rose before me was my fear. I drew back, made a sacrifice. The god welded this sword to my hand and infused my body with his power. I went in again. Deformed and terrifying denizens of the night seeped from the watery soil and glued themselves around me. They had bears' heads, camels' heads, turtles' heads, potlike paunches. They were somber, twisted, green with slime; a whole army of monsters at my command. I entered into the camp, slipping softly toward Dhristhadyumna's tent where, on rare carpets, my father's killer lay asleep. I kicked him awake, he tried to scream. I threw him to the ground, I crushed his throat with my knees. He tore at me with his nails. I killed him as one kills cattle.

DURYODHANA: Good, that's good. . . .

ASWATTHAMAN: Then I hurled myself into the camp. My force was superhuman, I massacred everyone. I killed Bhima's son, Arjuna's son, Yudhishthira's son, I killed the twins' sons. Draupadi hasn't one son left.

DURYODHANA: Yes, good, very good.

ASWATTHAMAN: I killed Sikhandin—I chopped him in two with my sword. I tore throats, I stabbed backs, I amputated heads, arms, ears. The joyful beasts of the night, their bellies swollen, crunched flesh and gulped down blood, repeating: "It's delicious, succulent, superb!" Then I withdrew in silence. I met Abhimanyu's young widow, I killed the fetus in her womb. The Pandavas have no more descendants. There. I have done what I needed to do. I am calm.

DURYODHANA: Good, very good. We will see one another again. . . . Now, I die.

*After the death of Duryodhana, the boy enters, alone, and approaches the body, not without fear.*

BOY: Vyasa . . . Vyasa . . .

VYASA: I am here.

*Vyasa appears. The boy goes up to him, reassured.*

BOY: Is the war over?

VYASA: Yes. The sun is slowly rising over eighteen million corpses. Birds of prey drag heroes by the feet. With cruel beaks they hack at mangled faces till the last mark of recognition goes. The beauty of a man leaves no trace in the beasts' jaws. *Karna, Abhimanyu, and another man appear, mutilated. They lie on the ground. They are dead. Vyasa says to the boy:*

VYASA: Don't be frightened. They don't see you anymore. *Women appear in the distance, looking for the bodies of their relatives.*

VYASA: The women stagger blindly in all directions. They grope for their children in the mud. Draupadi and Gandhari know that they will grow old without children. *The young wife of Abhimanyu goes and sits beside his body.*

VYASA: The young wife of Abhimanyu says to him: "For me, you are like riches in a dream. I see you; you are gone." *At this moment Bhishma enters. He is carried on his bed of arrows by the Pandavas and by Dhritarashtra who surround him, along with Sanjaya.*

BOY: Bhishma is still alive?

VYASA: Yes. He spoke for a long time to Yudhishthira from his bed of arrows. At the gate of death, he taught him the hard profession of kingship and the secret of the movements of mankind. He told him all that he had to tell. Then, the sun was ready to touch its zenith and Bhishma felt that his end was near.

*Kunti appears. She goes toward Karna's body.*

VYASA: As the sun pierced the bloodstained mist, Kunti, watched by everyone, went close to Karna's body. *Arjuna comes up to her.*

ARJUNA: Why are you kneeling beside Karna?

KUNTI: Karna—whom you killed—Karna was your eldest brother, my first son. I was fifteen years old.

ARJUNA: Karna was our brother?

KUNTI: Yes, Arjuna.

ARJUNA: He knew it?

KUNTI: Yes, he knew it.

ARJUNA: Why did you hide this from us?

KUNTI: Constantly hated by you—rejected, despised—he swore not to kill you, to spare you all, except you, Arjuna, so that after the battle I would have the same number of sons.

ARJUNA: You knew it, Krishna?

KRISHNA: Karna forbade me to reveal Kunti's secret to you. His promise was absolute.

ARJUNA: He preferred his word to his brothers?

KRISHNA: And you must respect his choice.

BHIMA: *To Kunti* He had the same feet as you. I often wondered why.

DHRITARASHTRA: *To Bhishma* This world is savage. How can one understand the savagery of this world?

BHISHMA: You are part of it.

DHRITARASHTRA: How can one escape? *Bhishma draws himself up.*

BHISHMA: A man is walking in a dark, dangerous forest, filled with wild beasts. The forest is surrounded by a vast net. The man is afraid, he runs to escape from the beasts, he falls into a pitch black hole. By a miracle, he is caught in some twisted roots. He feels the hot breath of an enormous snake, its jaws wide open, lying at the bottom of the pit. He is about to fall into these jaws. On the edge of the hole, a huge elephant is about to crush him. Black and white mice gnaw the roots from which the man is hanging. Dangerous bees fly over the hole letting fall drops of honey. . . . Then the man holds out his finger—slowly, cautiously—he holds out his finger to catch the drops of honey. Threatened by so many dangers, with hardly a breath between him and so many deaths, he still has not reached indifference. The thought of honey holds him to life.

DHRITARASHTRA: And you? Do you still wish for honey? *Bhishma does not reply.* Bhishma, answer me.

SANJAYA: His breath has left him. *Everyone bows down in grief. Then, suddenly, Yudhishthira rises and moves away.*

DRAUPADI: Where are you going?

YUDHISHTHIRA: I led my brother to his death. Now I'm going off into the woods.

DRAUPADI: And you give up your kingdom?

YUDHISHTHIRA: Yes, I will eat fruit and roots, I will wash twice a day, alone, without tears, without joy, an idiot, calm in the face, deaf and blind, wandering aimlessly, seeking neither death nor life.

ARJUNA: What's the sense, then, of this great battle?

DRAUPADI: Poverty is not glorious. Nor is sadness. Even deprived of my sons I want to live. What can I say to you, Yudhishthira? Must we tie you to the throne like a mad king?

YUDHISHTHIRA: Yes, Draupadi, I am mad, no one is madder than I am. I've killed your sons, I've killed millions of men.

DRAUPADI: Now I see you clearly. You were happy in the forest, you relished the taste of exile. You knew you were going to lose the game of dice—secretly you wanted to lose, you wanted to lose everything. When we left the city, barefoot, dragging ourselves behind you in misery, you were radiant, you had won.

DHRITARASHTRA: Yudhishthira, don't go. Don't despise this earth. I want you to revive our crippled kingdom.

VYASA: You are the most upright, you are the truest of men. And it needed exile, long suffering, this desperate war, and this harsh battle in yourself—and your lie and your anger and your delirium—it even needed wishing for your brother's blood for you now to be him whom the city awaits with all its garlands.

DHRITARASHTRA: Come into my arms. Come, have no fear. *Yudhish-thira goes forward. Dhritarashtra embraces him asking:* Is Bhima there?

BHIMA: Yes, I'm here.

DHRITARASHTRA: Come, I want to embrace you too. Come to me.

DHRITARASHTRA: Come, I want to embrace you too. Come to me. *Bhima goes toward the aged king but Krishna suddenly holds him back. He looks around him and picks up a dead body with Bhima's help. They carry it while Dhritarashtra gets impatient.* Where are you? Come, I want to hold you in my arms!

BHIMA: I am here.

DHRITARASHTRA: Where?

BHIMA: Here, before you. *At the last moment Krishna substitutes the dead body for Bhima. Dhritarashtra takes it in his arms.*

DHRITARASHTRA: Bhima, how hard you are. I was afraid of you for so long. *Dhritarashtra squeezes with all his strength.* Ah, Bhima . . . *Dhritarashtra drops the body. He totters with fatigue, overcome by his effort. Almost unconscious, he sobs:* I've killed him, I've killed him.

KRISHNA: No, you haven't killed him; I saw deep anger burning in you and I kept him away.

DHRITARASHTRA: I felt his bones break.

KRISHNA: It was a dead man you crushed in your arms. *Bhima raises Dhritarashtra. Krishna then says to Gandhari:* You too Gandhari, take care. Wipe away the words you're about to utter.

GANDHARI: I can only think through pain. Bhima killed my son ignobly. I can't understand his treacherous blow.

BHIMA: I hadn't an atom of strength left in me.

GANDHARI: And Dushassana's blood? How could you drink it?

BHIMA: The blood never got past my lips and teeth.

GANDHARI: Why not have left me one son? Just one son? Where is Yudhishthira?

YUDHISHTHIRA: Here.

YUDHISHTHIRA: Don't blame Bhima for your son's death. I am responsible. Ah! *He gives a cry of pain and holds his foot.*

DRAUPADI: What hit you?

KRISHNA: It's the look in Gandhari's eyes. It passed under her band; it fell on his foot and was so charged with grief that it burned him. *Gandhari then addresses Krishna:*

GANDHARI: Krishna, you didn't keep your word. You took part in the battle with weapons more terrible than all the others. You rejoiced in our misfortune; you watched my son die like a spectator. Krishna, I curse you: one day, all that you are building will crumble; your friends will be massacred by your friends; dry blood will coat the walls of your dead city where only vultures reign; your shattered heart will mourn; you will leave, solitary; a passerby will kill you.

KRISHNA: Yes, Gandhari, what you see is true. I know. But even if you can't see it, a light has been saved. *Yudhishthira makes a sudden decision:*

YUDHISHTHIRA: Come with me. *He leaves first. The living and the dead follow him.*

# KRISHNA'S DEATH

*Watching Yudhishthira leave, Krishna asks Vyasa:*

KRISHNA: Vyasa, they're all leaving. Do you want me to stay with you?

VYASA: You must stay.

KRISHNA: What role have you in store for me now?

VYASA: You know well.

BOY: *To Krishna* Are you going to die too?

KRISHNA: Yes, of course. Like any other life, time has fixed my limit.

BOY: *To Vyasa* Are they all going to die without children?

VYASA: Yes, all of them.

BOY: But you told me, "This poem tells the story of your race." Am I born from a dead race? *Abhimanyu's young widow has held back for a moment. She goes out slowly. Krishna indicates her to the boy:*

KRISHNA: Look at this woman. She was Abhimanyu's wife and she bears his child. At his birth he will be dead, but I will restore him to life because his blood is the blood of Arjuna, my friend. Centuries and centuries will go by and you will come from this woman. *They watch the woman who is looking at them. She leaves. Krishna says to the boy:* This will be my last action. Later—thirty-six years later— terrible convulsions will tear my kingdom apart. Then I'll remember Gandhari's words and I'll say to myself: "The moment has come. I

230

must go into the forest alone and die on the spot where I drop with fatigue." *He has started walking. Exhausted, he falls to the ground and lies on his back. He sleeps. At once, a hunter enters. He sees Krishna's feet and shoots an arrow at them. Krishna sits up with a cry. The hunter approaches and recognizes him.*

HUNTER: Krishna, is it you? In the gloom of the forest, I mistook your feet for the ears of a deer. Forgive me.

KRISHNA: There's no cause for concern. I die, it's as it should be. *The boy rushes to Krishna:*

BOY: Krishna, I've so many things to ask you.

KRISHNA: Tell me, quickly.

BOY: Why all your tricks? And your bad directions?

KRISHNA: I fought against terrible powers and I did what I could.

BOY: What was it you said to Arjuna before the battle?

KRISHNA: I showed him the path of freedom, of true, right action. But he's forgotten it all.

BOY: What freedom, what path?

KRISHNA: These are very difficult questions and I can never say anything twice.

BOY: Please! *Krishna does not answer. He is still. Vyasa moves the boy away saying:*

VYASA: Krishna's no longer with us. *They carry Krishna away.*

# BY THE RIVER

*Kunti, Gandhari, and Dhritarashtra appear, covered in the dust of a long journey.*

GANDHARI: Are we in the forest?

KUNTI: Yes.

GANDHARI: I hear a river.

KUNTI: Yes, there, close by.

GANDHARI: No one has followed us?

KUNTI: I see no one.

GANDHARI: We're going to live our last days here, without any fear of death.

DHRITARASHTRA: It's good when kings finish their lives in solitude.

GANDHARI: Thirty-six years have gone by since the great battle and I still hear the crash of steel and the cry of flesh.

KUNTI: Krishna's dead. Last night there were rings of light around the moon.

GANDHARI: And what else?

KUNTI: An iron sky struck with lightning; rivers twisting out of course.

GANDHARI: Winds stronger each day.

KUNTI: Rats multiply, they chew people's hair in their sleep. Food in the kitchens is crawling with worms. Flames curve to the left. *Gandhari sighs. Dhritarashtra asks her:*

DHRITARASHTRA: You sighed, Gandhari. Are you sad?

GANDHARI: It wasn't a sigh of sadness. All the odors here bring back my childhood.

DHRITARASHTRA: Each day you must have regretted the fair land of your birth.

GANDHARI: No, the day I married you I killed every other thought.

DHRITARASHTRA: I don't believe you. *Gandhari remains silent and Dhritarashtra says:* You were cheated. You were married without being told I was blind. I destroyed your life.

GANDHARI: At first you thought that I couldn't hold out, that I'd take off the band. You could have ordered me to take it off. You were the king, you could have said to me, "At least look at your children." But you never said it.

DHRITARASHTRA: I felt your anger. I always felt it close to me. I still feel it. *Gandhari says nothing.* Our life is nearly over. Take off your band.

GANDHARI: No.

DHRITARASHTRA: You can't die with your eyes closed. Take off your band. It's an order. *Gandhari stands but does not take off the band.* Have you taken it off?

GANDHARI: Yes.

DHRITARASHTRA: What can you see?

GANDHARI: I can't see anything clearly. My eyes must get accustomed to the light.

DHRITARASHTRA: And now?

GANDHARI: Yes, I begin to distinguish shapes, trees, the sky, two birds go by. *She goes to Kunti.* It's you, Kunti?

KUNTI: Yes, it's me.

GANDHARI: I've never seen you.

KUNTI: I've never known the look in your eyes. *Gandhari cries:*

GANDHARI: Ah!

DHRITARASHTRA: What?

GANDHARI: I've just seen a whole army rise out of the river. All my sons, smiling, their wounds healed, reconciled. An immense wave of men, all white, mounting into the air. I can't see them anymore. The river is quietly closing again.

DHRITARASHTRA: There's a fire somewhere in the forest.

GANDHARI: Yes, since morning I've felt the smoke. I hear animals crying as they run away.

KUNTI: The fire's coming toward us. *A short silence. Fire rises.*

GANDHARI: It's easier than I thought to hold your hand up to the end.

DHRITARASHTRA: Dive into the river.

GANDHARI: I feel the fire's breath.

DHRITARASHTRA: Cross the river, save your life! *Gandhari draws him toward the forest.*

GANDHARI: Come, let's both walk toward the flame. Put your hand on my shoulder. *Dhritarashtra follows her without speaking. She says to Kunti:* And you, Kunti, if you wish, come with us. *Kunti accompanies them.*

    *All three go to meet the fire.*

# THE LAST ILLUSION

*Yudhishthira appears, aged, shivering with cold, exhausted by a long climb. He holds a dog in his arms. An imperious voice, that of Vyasa, asks:*

MESSENGER: Who has come as far as this? Who are you?

YUDHISHTHIRA: I am Yudhishthira. I am looking for the gate of paradise.

MESSENGER: It's here. Are you alone?

YUDHISHTHIRA: Yes, we decided to leave the earth, my brothers and Draupadi, but while climbing the mountain they slipped. One after the other they fell into the abyss—the twins, Draupadi, even Arjuna, even Bhima. I've come here alone.

MESSENGER: Your kingdom has known thirty-six years of happiness. You have proved yourself to be the best of kings, your place is amongst us. Leave this dog and enter.

YUDHISHTHIRA: I can't leave this dog.

MESSENGER: Why?

YUDHISHTHIRA: He's followed me ever since I left the city.

MESSENGER: Dogs don't enter here. Leave him.

YUDHISHTHIRA: No. He's come all this way with me, we go in together.

MESSENGER: Paradise isn't open to dogs! Leave him behind, it's no cruelty. Your brothers are here already. Enter, come and join them, leave this dog.

YUDHISHTHIRA: Abandon a creature who loves me, who's alone and defenseless? I can't.

MESSENGER: You've given up everything, give up this dog. Otherwise you won't pass this door.

YUDHISHTHIRA: I'll stay outside in the icy wind with this dog. *The Guardian–Messenger—who is, in fact, Vyasa—invites Yudhishthira to enter saying:*

VYASA: Enter. The dog is another form of Dharma, your father. Once, a long time ago, he took the shape of a lake, you remember? He has always followed and observed you. Enter the inconceivable region with him.

YUDHISHTHIRA: Can I go in with my body?

VYASA: Yes, come. *Yudhishthira steps over the threshold of paradise. Suddenly Duryodhana appears before him, smiling, splendidly dressed, accompanied by Dushassana, also smiling. They are holding cups of wine.*

YUDHISHTHIRA: Is that Duryodhana?

VYASA: Yes.

YUDHISHTHIRA: He's here?

VYASA: He's here with his brothers, with all his family.

YUDHISHTHIRA: Millions of men died because of him and he's here? He drinks? He smiles? He seems happy?

VYASA: He is happy. He's calm. Here, all hates vanish. Kiss him!

YUDHISHTHIRA: Don't ask me to kiss him. I can't. If this murderer is here, where are my brothers? Where is our wife? What is paradise if I'm separated from my family? I want to see them!

VYASA: I'll show them to you, follow me. *Yudhishthira follows the Messenger who draws him into ever deeper darkness.*

YUDHISHTHIRA: Where are you taking me?

VYASA: To where your brothers are. Come.

YUDHISHTHIRA: Where is this pathway leading? The stench is dreadful, it's all black, the mist smells of putrefaction.

VYASA: Follow me.

YUDHISHTHIRA: I see scraps of flesh, blood. . . .

VYASA: Be very careful, one can meet enormous bears here and birds with iron beaks.

YUDHISHTHIRA: They're like amputated limbs, bleeding guts. Where are we? Where are my brothers?

VYASA: Farther still. I'm stopping here. Go on a bit. If the smell upsets you, you can turn back with me. *Lamentations rise from the shadow. Yudhishthira listens.*

KARNA'S VOICE: Yudhishthira, don't go.

DRAUPADI'S VOICE: Stay with us!

BHIMA'S VOICE: You bring us a fresh breeze.

ARJUNA'S VOICE: Stay!

DRAUPADI'S VOICE: Our pains are lighter when you are here.

YUDHISHTHIRA: Who are you? Who's speaking?

KARNA: Don't you know me? I'm Karna. Your brother.

ARJUNA: I'm Arjuna

BHIMA: I'm Bhima

NAKULA: I'm Nakula

SAHADEVA: I'm Sahadeva

DRAUPADI: I'm Draupadi. We're all here. *Yudhishthira sees them, recognizes them.*

YUDHISHTHIRA: You! Here! Tortured! In this rotten smell of corpses! Who decided this? Am I awake? Am I conscious or unconscious? Is this a disorder of the brain? What act have these beings commited to be thrown down into Hell? I will stay here, since I've seen that my presence brings comfort to my family. I condemn the Gods. I condemn Dharma. Tell the Gods I will never go up there again. *Vyasa gently goes to Yudhishthira while Ganesha reappears with his writing materials.*

VYASA: Then the keeper of the last dwelling said to Yudhishthira: "Stop shouting. You've known neither paradise nor hell. Here, there is no happiness, no punishment, no family, no enemies. Rise in tranquillity. Here, words end, like thought. This was the last illusion." *Ganesha repeats as he finishes writing:*

GANESHA: This was the last illusion. *Yudhishthira looks around him in astonishment. He sees his brothers, Draupadi, and Kunti smiling, intact. The other characters reappear, calm and relaxed.*

*Dhritarashtra has gained his sight and Gandhari has taken off her band.*

*For an instant they wash in the river, then sit beside the musicians, who play as the story comes to its end. Refreshments are handed around. They are slowly enveloped by the night.*

## About the Author and Translator

Jean-Claude Carrière has written some forty films, fifteen books and twelve plays, and worked closely with directors Jacques Tati, Louis Malle, Pierre Etaix, Marco Ferreri, Milos Forman, Volker Schlondorff, Andrey Wajda, and Luis Buñuel. His films include *The Discreet Charm of the Bourgeoisie* and *The Tin Drum* (both of which won Oscars for Best Foreign Film), *Belle de Jour*, *The Milky Way*, *That Obscure Object of Desire*, *Taking Off*, *Danton*, and *The Return of Martin Guerre*. He has worked with Peter Brook since 1974, collaborating on seven plays, including *The Conference of the Birds*, *The Tragedy of Carmen*, and *The Mahabharata*.

He lives in Paris and is president of the New French School for Cinema and Television (FEMIS).

Peter Brook has been a director of the Royal Shakespeare Company, and currently heads the International Centre of Theatre Research in Paris. Among over fifty productions, he has directed *Love's Labours Lost*, *The Tempest*, and *King Lear* in Stratford upon Avon; *Ring Around the Moon*, *Oedipus*, *A View from the Bridge*, and *Hamlet* in London; *The Visit*, *Marat/Sade*, *A Midsummer Night's Dream*, and *The Tragedy of Carmen* in New York; *Sergeant Musgrave's Dance*, *The Conference of the Birds*, *Timon of Athens*, and *The Cherry Orchard* in Paris. His films include *Lord of the Flies*, *King Lear*, and *Meetings with Remarkable Men*, among others. His operas include *The Marriage of Figaro* and *Boris Gudonov* at Covent Garden, and *Faust* and *Eugene Onegin* at the Metropolitan Opera.

He has written many articles, and *The Empty Space*, published in 1968. He currently lives in Paris.